What is
Historical Sociology?

This book is dedicated to my aunt, Ruth Becker,
who always has encouraged my intellectual curiosity.

Contents

Acknowledgments

I appreciate the helpful advice offered by Georgi Derluguian, Roberto Franzosi, anonymous reviewers, and my editor at Polity, Jonathan Skerrett. I especially thank Rebecca Emigh for her detailed suggestions for revisions.

Brief portions of chapter 2 previously appeared in "Class Formation without Class Struggle: An Elite Theory of the Transition to Capitalism," *American Sociological Review*, 5(3), 1990, pp. 398–414; in "Comparisons within a Single Social Formation: A Critical Appreciation of Perry Anderson's Lineages of the Absolutist State," *Qualitative Sociology*, 25(1), 2002, pp. 83–92; and in *States and Power* (Polity, 2010); of chapter 4 in "Comments," pp. 22–4 in "Book Symposium on James Mahoney's Colonialism and Post-Colonial Development: Spanish America in Comparative Perspective," in *Trajectories: Newsletter of the ASA Comparative Historical Sociology Section* of the American Sociological Association, 23(2), 2012; and of chapter 8 in *States and Power* (Polity 2010) and in "Read This Book! The World Republic of Letters, Pascale Casanova," in *Trajectories: Newsletter of the ASA Comparative Historical Sociology Section*, 18(1), 2006, pp. 15–16.

1
The Sense of a Beginning

Sociology was created to explain historical change. Sociology's founders were convinced they were living through a social transformation that was unprecedented in human history, and that a new discipline was needed to describe and analyze that change, explain its origins, and explore its implications for human existence. As Tocqueville ([1835] 2003, p. 16) put it, "A new political science is needed for a totally new world." The founders disagreed over the nature of that change and over how their discipline should go about studying it. They also were not sure if the theories they developed to explain their own epoch of change could be used to develop a general "science of society." Nevertheless, they all – Marx, Weber, Durkheim, and their less illustrious contemporaries – saw the new discipline of sociology as historical.

Sociology at its beginning was historical because of the questions its founders asked.

For Marx the key questions were: What is capitalism, why did it supplant other social systems, and how is it transforming the ways in which people work, reproduce themselves biologically and socially, and gain knowledge and exploit the natural world? What effect do those changes have on relations of power, domination, and exploitation?

Weber also asked about epochal historical shifts. He sought to explain the origins of world religions, of capitalism, and of rational action, and to see how that species of rationality affected the exercise of power, the development of science (including social science), religion, and the humanities, the organization of work, government, markets and families, and pretty much everything else humans did.

Durkheim asked how the division of labor, and the historical shift from mechanical to organic solidarity, changed the organization of workplaces, schools, families, communities, and entire societies, and affected nations' capacities to wage wars.[1]

Since its beginnings as a historical discipline concerned with epochal social transformation, sociology has become increasingly focused on the present day and on trying to explain individual behavior. Like the children's book *All About Me* (Kranz 2004), in which pages are set aside for their young owners to write about what they like to do in their "favorite place," to describe their hobby, or to "name three things that make you feel important," many sociologists, especially in the United States, look to their personal biographies or their immediate environs to find research topics. Take a look at the program of the annual meeting of the American Sociological Association. It contains sociology's version of the ages of man. First we are born, and legions of demographers explain why our mothers had us when they were 26.2 instead of 25.8 years old. We become sexually aware and active, and there are sociologists who keep on reliving their teen years in research on losing virginity or coming out of the closet. As adults, we have criminologists to tell us which ghetto youth will mug us and which will become a nerd in his failed urban school. The medical sociologists can tell us why we will be overmedicated and overbilled in our dotage. And most of this research is ahistorical and non-comparative, focused on the United States in the last five minutes.

Meanwhile, in the larger world, fundamental transformations are underway: the world's population grew to unprecedented levels in the past century, even as those billions of people consumed resources at a pace the global ecosystem cannot sustain. Soon whole countries will run out of water or be submerged under rising seas. Global warming will force mass migrations on a scale never seen in human history. Governments lack the organizational capacity and almost certainly the desire to accommodate those refugees; many, however, will have the military means and popular support to repel needy migrants.

Today service jobs are following manufacturing and agriculture in being replaced by machines, creating the possibility that most human labor will no longer be needed to sustain current or future levels of production (Collins forthcoming; Brynjolfssom and McAfee 2012). The nature of war also is being transformed. Mass conscription – which originated at the end of the eighteenth century, made possible wars between armies with millions of soldiers, and encouraged states to develop weapons capable both of killing thousands of enemy fighters at a time and of targeting the civilian populations that manufactured the weapons and provided the recruits for those armies – has over the past half-century been abolished in almost all Western nations, which now either no longer fight wars or attempt to rely on high-tech weaponry.

Inequality within the wealthiest countries of the world has risen rapidly in the last three decades after declining for the previous four decades, while at the same time some of the countries that before World War II had been dominated by the US and Europe and were mired in poverty have achieved high levels of geopolitical autonomy and are rapidly closing the economic gap with the West. Ever fewer people on this planet live in communities that are isolated from the rest of the world, and the population of farmers that dwindled to a tiny fraction of the people living in rich countries is now rapidly declining in most of the rest of the world. For the first time in human history a majority of the world's population lives in urban areas. Links of exploitation that were established, as Marx first explained, with the advent of capitalism now are joined with various sorts of communicative links that hold the potential for more egalitarian relations within and among nations.

Sociology is especially equipped, analytically and methodologically, to analyze the implications of these early twenty-first-century transformations, just as it was created to explain the complex of disruptive and unprecedented changes that accompanied the advent of modern capitalist societies. But sociology can help us understand what is most significant and consequential about our contemporary world only when it is historical sociology. As Craig Calhoun (2003, p. 383) rightly notes: "The most compelling reason for the existence of historical sociology is embarrassingly obvious (embarrassingly because so often ignored). This is the importance of studying social change."

My goal in this book is to turn our attention away from the sort of solipsistic and small-bore research that is presented in sociology textbooks, and which dominates too many of the major academic journals, and focus instead on understanding how sociological analyses of historical change can allow us to understand both the origins of our contemporary world and the scope and consequences of current transformations. Since much of that research is confined today to the subfield of historical sociology, this then has to be a book that examines what is historical sociology. My hope is that historical sociology's concerns, methods, and understandings can invigorate the broader discipline of sociology, making it once again a discipline about social change rather than one that confines itself to models and ethnographic descriptions of static social relations.

This book, and historical sociology, will not help you learn all about you. Historical sociology can help you understand the world in which you will live your life. It provides context to determine the magnitude and significance of present-day changes in gender relations, family structure, and demographic patterns, and in the organization and content of work, the economy, culture, politics, and international relations. Because historical sociology is inherently comparative, we can see what is unusual about any particular society, including our own, at each moment in time and to distinguish mere novelties from fundamental social change.

If the sociology envisioned by its founders is very different from much of contemporary sociology, that early sociology was also distinguished from the history written by historians. Since Marx, Weber, and Durkheim were trying to explain a single unprecedented social transformation, they ended up slighting and even ignoring the bulk of the world's history that occurred before the modern era. They also decided what history to study, and how to understand the historical evidence they examined, deductively – in terms of the meta-theories and master concepts they advanced. That led them to rummage through the works of numerous historians, often taking the latter's findings out of context to construct broad arguments about social change. Professional historians, not surprisingly, found it easy to ignore sociological theories that floated above, and failed to engage, the archival evidence and the specific times and places upon which they define themselves and engage with one another. As a result, Weber and Durkheim and their theories have had little influence on historians.

Durkheim has been easy for historians to ignore, since he almost never referred to or engaged specific historical events. Weber, who drew on a vast range of historical research, has suffered because virtually every contemporary historian of the Reformation rejects his most famous work, *The Protestant Ethic and the Spirit of Capitalism*. Fernand Braudel (1977, pp. 65–6) accurately summarizes his profession's judgment: "All historians have opposed this tenuous theory, although they have not managed to be rid of it once and for all. Yet it is clearly false." As a result, historians are not inclined to look to Weber for theoretical or empirical guidance on other historical changes.

Marx has faired better among historians, perhaps because they do not regard him as a sociologist. Yet, historians who define themselves as Marxist, or who seek to draw on elements of Marxism, for the most part use Marx to inform their studies of specific historical eras and problems. Few historians see themselves as contributors to Marx's overarching project of explaining the origins of capitalism or tracing the dynamics of capitalism on a global or even a national scale.

Marx, Weber, and Durkheim's theories also have been challenged by non-European scholars (and by Western scholars aware of the histories and intellectual traditions of the rest of the world) who doubt that the transformation those theories are designed to explain was "anything like a 'universal human history' " (Chakrabarty 2007, p. 3). Instead, Chakrabarty, like other "post-colonial" scholars, sees those early sociological theories and much of what Europeans and North Americans have written since as "histories that belonged to the multiple pasts of Europe . . . drawn from very particular intellectual and historical traditions that could not claim any universal validity" (ibid., p. xiii). Or, as Michael Dutton (2005, p. 89) puts it, "Why is it that, when it comes to Asian area studies, whenever 'theory' is invoked, it is invariably understood to mean 'applied theory' and assumed to be of value only insofar as it helps tell the story of the 'real' in a more compelling way?" One of my goals in this book is to explore the extent to which "Western" historical sociology can address social change elsewhere in the world, and also to see how theories and research from the "rest" of the world can inform, deepen, and challenge sociology from and about Europe.

Historical sociologists in recent decades have worked to narrow the distance between their scholarship and that of historians. Yet, the two disciplines have not merged. An aspiring academic's decision to study and pursue a career in historical sociology rather than history still has implications for what sort of intellectual they will become and what sort of research they will undertake. While historical sociologists and historians do interact with each other, they still spend most of their time learning from and seeking to address scholars in their own discipline. That matters because history and sociology have their own histories, and the past intellectual, institutional, and career decisions made by historians and sociologists shape the questions asked, the methods employed, the data analyzed, and the arguments offered within each discipline today. While there are many historians whose work influences sociologists, and some historical sociologists who have won the respect of sociologists, in practice scholars in the two disciplines study history in quite different ways. Often undergraduate and even graduate students are not much aware of those differences and may decide which field to pursue without considering all the implications of their choice. I wrote this book in part to clarify what it means to do historical sociology so that readers who are considering studying that field will have a clear idea of what it is like to pursue an academic career as a historical sociologist.

Charles Tilly offers an apt and accurate generalization of historians: they share an "insistence on time and place as fundamental principles of variation" (1991, p. 87) – e.g., the eighteenth-century French Revolution is very different, because it was earlier and in a different part of the world, from the twentieth-century Chinese Revolution. As a result most historians are recognized and define themselves by the particular time and place they study, and organize their careers around that temporal and geographic specialization. The boundaries of those specializations coincide with and "are firmly embedded in institutional practices that invoke the nation-state at every step – witness the organization and politics of teaching, recruitment, promotions, and publication in history departments" worldwide (Chakrabarty 2007, p. 41). Today, most academic historians everywhere in the world are hired as historians of nineteenth-century US history, Renaissance Italian history, twentieth-century Chinese history, or some other such temporal-geographic specialization. Usually, history departments will hire more specialists, and make finer distinctions, for the history of their own country than for the rest of the world. Thus a US history department might have a specialist in the military history of the Civil War among a dozen Americanists along with a single historian of China, while in China a department might have one or two Americanists along with a dozen historians who each specialize in a single dynasty.

Historians' country specializations make sense because they "anchor . . . most of [their] dominant questions in national politics," which leads historians to use "documentary evidence . . . [for the] identification of crucial actors [and the] imputation of attitudes and motives to those actors" (Tilly 1991, pp. 87–8). Historians' country specializations, in turn, influence and limit when and how they go about making comparisons across time periods and geographic spaces. "[H]istorians are not accustomed, or indeed trained, to make grand comparisons or even to work with general concepts, and they often view the whole past through the lens of the particular period in which they have specialized" (Burke 2003, p. 59).

Immanuel Wallerstein offers a wonderful example of how national categories shape historical thinking in an essay entitled "Does India Exist?" ([1986] 2000). Wallerstein notes that what today is India was an amalgamation of separate territories, created by British colonization in the eighteenth and nineteenth centuries. India's political, and also cultural, unity is an artifact of Britain's ability to colonize the entire subcontinent. Wallerstein poses

> a counterfactual proposition. Suppose . . . the British colonized primarily the old Mughal Empire, calling it Hindustan, and the French had simultaneously colonized the southern (largely Dravidian) zones of the present-day Republic of India, giving it the name Dravidia. Would we today think that Madras was "historically" part of India: Would we even use the word "India"? . . . Instead, probably, scholars from around the world would have written learned tomes, demonstrating from time immemorial "Hindustan" and "Dravidia" were two different cultures, peoples, civilizations, nations, or whatever. (Ibid., p. 310)

India's present-day unity is a combined creation of British colonization, the nationalist resistance to British rule, and the inability of other imperial powers (such as France, which tried and failed) to grab part of the subcontinent for themselves. Wallerstein's point is that a contingent series of events, and non-events that failed to occur, created both a political unit and an academic terrain (the study of India) that affects not just scholarship about the era that began with British colonization but also historical and cultural studies of the centuries before then, when a unified Indian polity or culture did not yet exist. Had the contingencies of the past three centuries played out differently, not only would the present-day reality be different, but so would historians' retrospective reading of the distant past.

Historical sociologists, in contrast, organize their research and careers around theoretical questions – e.g., what are the causes of revolutions, what explains the variation in social benefits offered by governments to their citizens, how and why have family structures changed over time? These questions, like Marx, Weber, and Durkheim's questions about social change in the modern era, cannot be answered with a focus on a single era in a single nation. History itself, thus, matters in very different ways in historians and sociologists' explanations. For example, historians are skeptical that knowledge gained about how French people acted during their revolution in 1789 is of much help in understanding how the Chinese acted in 1949 during their revolution.

Historical sociologists instead see each revolution as the culmination of a chain of events that open certain opportunities for action while foreclosing others. Thus, to a sociologist, both the French in 1789 and the Chinese in 1949 gained the opportunity to make their revolutions as a result of previous events that created certain social structures and social relations and ended others. Historical sociologists focus their attention on comparing the structures and events of those, and other, revolutions. What is distinctive about each is secondary, in sociological analysis, to what is similar. Sociologists analyze differences systematically in an effort to find patterns that can account for each outcome. The goal, for sociologists, is to construct theories that can explain ever more cases and account for both similarities and variations.

The differences between history and historical sociology, thus, are grounded in the ways in which those two disciplines have developed. However, it would be a mistake to advance an essentialist argument about the differences between history and historical sociology. Practitioners of both disciplines would agree with Charles Tilly's (1991, p. 86) contention: "To the degree that social processes are path-dependent – to the extent that the prior sequence of events constrains what happens at a given point in time – historical knowledge of sequences becomes essential." In other words, historians and historical sociologists both devote themselves to explaining how social actors are constrained by what they and their predecessors did in earlier times. As Marx put it in his greatest work of historical analysis, *The Eighteenth Brumaire of Louis Bonaparte* ([1852] 1963, p. 15), "Men make their own history, but they do not make it just as they please; they do not make it under circumstances chosen by themselves, but under circumstances encountered, given and transmitted from the past."

Marx was expressing what Philip Abrams, a historian, describes as the "two-sidedness of the social world . . . a world of which we are both creators and the creatures" (1982, p. 2). We construct historical explanations of how we are creatures of the actions that humans took in the past to form the social world we inhabit and which in so many ways constrains our desires, beliefs, choices, and actions. At the same time, we are actors who are making history, creating a new social order in the spaces for transformative action that exist in our world. Both how we are constrained and the opportunities we have for transformative action are historically determined. Our constraints and opportunities are different from those of people who lived before us, and our actions ensure that the possibilities for action in the future will be different yet again. That is why Abrams (ibid.) is justified in asserting: "Sociological explanation is necessarily historical. Historical sociology is thus not some special kind of sociology; rather, it is the essence of the discipline."

Not all actions are equal. "Most happenings reproduce social and cultural structures without significant change. Events may be defined as that relatively rare subclass of happenings that significantly transform structures. An eventful conception of temporality, therefore, is one that takes into account the transformation of structures by events" (Sewell 1996, p. 262). Abrams (1982, p. 191) uses the same word, "event," to identify "a portentous outcome; it is a transformation device between past and future."

Historical sociological explanations, therefore, need to do the following:

- first, to distinguish inconsequential everyday human actions from the rare moments when people transformed social structure;
- second, to explain why transformative events occur at particular times and places and not elsewhere;
- third, to show how events make possible later events.

When historical sociology undertakes these three tasks, it is engaged in what Abbott (1992, p. 68) describes as "the case/ narrative approach," which he contrasts to the "population/ analytic" approach. The population/analytic approach is dominant in sociology: it treats "all included variables as equally salient" – i.e., its goal is to measure the relative influence of many variables across numerous cases. The case/ narrative approach pays attention to variables only when they matter in the causal sequence that produces the outcome that we want to explain. "This selective attention goes along with an emphasis on contingency. Things happen because of constellations of factors, not because of a few fundamental effects acting independently." Contingency is the key word. Nothing is inevitable or predetermined. Events become significant when they produce other events that in a cumulative chain transform social reality.[2]

An event's significance is "established primarily in terms of its location in time, in relation to a course or chain of other happenings" (Abrams 1982 p. 191). A similar event – a famine, a war, a revolution, or the establishment of a social benefit – can have very different consequences, and also different causes, depending on its place in a sequence of events. Let's look at three examples of how timing and sequence matter:

1 The French, Russian, and Chinese revolutions occurred after some events (defeats in war, agrarian crises, and successful resistance by the landlord class to reforms) and before other events (the expropriation of landlords' property and political power, the creation of powerful centralized states). Theda Skocpol (1979) argued that all three revolutions were caused by the set of events that occurred beforehand, and that the revolutions made possible the events that occurred afterwards. However, Sewell (1996) notes that certain other events, such as the Industrial Revolution and the creation of a proletariat, occurred before the Russian but not the French Revolution. Sewell contends that the presence of a proletariat made the Russian Revolution substantially different from the French, and meant that the Soviet revolutionary regime was able to accomplish things (for good or evil) that the French revolutionary state could not. Adding an event into a contingent chain of events alters subsequent events substantially.[3]

2 In the two decades from 1945 to 1965, almost all British and French colonies won independence. Variation in the post-independence regimes was due in large part to events that occurred before independence: whether nationalists mounted an armed struggle against the colonial power, what sort of economy developed under colonialism, and even what type of economy had existed before Europeans colonized those lands, in some cases centuries earlier.

3   As I wrote this book in 2012, the United States was finally about to join every other wealthy industrialized country in the world and institute a system of nationally guaranteed health insurance for its citizens. Plans to create that social benefit were proposed repeatedly throughout the twentieth century, but never enacted. In the absence of a national health-care system, American insurance and drug companies, hospitals, and the medical profession itself developed in a very different way than was the case in all the countries that had established a national insurance system. As a result, the US national benefit, finally legislated under President Obama, had to take a very different form and will have different and narrower effects on the actual delivery and cost of health care than if the political support to enact such legislation had come together in earlier decades.

American medical costs are likely to remain higher, and health outcomes poorer, than in other countries that created their national systems earlier. Thus, if a medical sociologist wants to explain why the US is now thirty-fourth among nations in life expectancy, despite spending 16 percent of GDP on health care, which is more than 50 percent higher than any other country in the world (Jacobs and Skocpol 2010, p. 21 and *passim*), the answer will not be found in static comparisons among systems, or just by focusing on demographic differences among populations, or by highlighting Americans' supposed excessive proclivities to seek medical care. Rather, the differences will be found in the events that created particular American medical institutions in the long decades before a national system was created in the twenty-first century.

We will have much more to say about how historical sociology addresses revolutions, empires, and states in subsequent chapters. The general point that I want to draw from these examples here is that we can understand how humans make and change their world, and identify cause and effect, only in temporal sequence. We need to know what happened first – in other words, we need to study history, to determine causality. All valid theoretical claims must be grounded in a careful conception of how temporal sequences are formed and how they matter.

We will gain a clearer understanding of how time matters, and learn how we can be precise about the ways in which time structures human choices and limits, by looking at historical sociologists' writings in a range of substantive areas. Contemporary historical sociologists, unlike the founders of sociology, have been highly successful at combining serious contributions to historical analysis with the progressive elaboration of theory. We can best understand how to do historical sociology, and to appreciate what historical sociology has to offer, by examining exemplary works (exemplary both for their achievements and for their limitations and failings).

Chapter 2 will look at how historical sociologists analyze the original problem that Marx and Weber thought was at the core of sociology: the origins of capitalism. Marx and Weber, as well as their successors, have disagreed in part because they define capitalism in different ways. Those disagreements, in turn, lead them to differ on when and where capitalism began, and therefore to identify different events and trajectories of change that culminated in that transformation. As we adjudicate among these competing definitions and explanations, we will see how historical sociologists go about constructing theories and engage in historical analysis.

Chapter 3 examines how to study sudden historical change through the analysis of revolutions and social movements. Again, we will be concerned with origins and trajectories, but we will also see how sociologists try to understand why the pace of social change can suddenly accelerate, and why human agency becomes more effective in certain times and places.

If revolutions give the oppressed new social power, empires have the opposite effect: subjugating entire peoples to foreign rulers. Chapter 4 examines domination on the largest scale. We will see how sociologists try to account for the emergence, endurance, and disappearance of empires. This will also allow us to evaluate Chakrabarty's assertion (noted above) that theories developed to explain historical change in the West cannot be used uncritically to examine social change in other parts of the world.

The entire globe (except Antarctica) is divided into sovereign states. States will make repeated appearances throughout this book as sites of capitalist development, the cores and components of empires, and the targets of social movements. Much historical sociology takes the state itself as the object of study. Historical sociology offers a very different understanding of the events that are key bailiwicks of history: wars, dynastic change, and elections. By exploring how sociologists have studied state formation, we will be able, in chapter 5, to clarify historical sociology's approach to those sorts of events and the data they generate. We will see how sociologists have constructed meta-narratives of the historical development of war and nationalism. Finally, that chapter will show how sociologists construct historical explanations for the development and divergence of social welfare systems across the world.

Inequality is one of the main topics of sociological investigation, but most of that research is ahistorical and non-comparative. At the same time, historians tend to address inequality in impressionistic and non-quantitative ways. Historical sociologists have been able to advance both disciplines' agendas and approaches to inequality. We will see how they have done that in chapter 6.

Chapter 7 will examine how historical sociology addresses gender. One of the hallmarks of gender studies since its beginning has been to show how gender is malleable and changeable. Historical sociologists bring precision to that insight, as they trace the transformation of gender relations over time. We also will see how they link the study of gender to the examination of changes in household form and dynamics and to state policies.

Historical sociology, like much of the rest of sociology, has taken a cultural turn. That turn, traced and celebrated by Adams, Clemens, and Orloff (2005), will have emerged at various points in the previous chapters. My concern in chapter 8 is with how historical sociologists make culture itself a subject and causal force in their explanations. Much recent American cultural sociology is focused on the contemporary US and has proceeded in almost total ignorance of decades of cultural studies in Europe. My goal in this chapter is to show how cultural history contributes to our understanding of the debates and subjects of the previous chapters and also constitutes itself as a vital subject of study.

The theories and methods that sociologists developed to study historical change also can be, and have been, used to offer predictions about the future. In chapter 9, which concludes this book, we will see how techniques of counterfactual history can be turned to study the future. Our understandings of capitalism, states, and empires as social systems provide the bases to predict the sources and course of future crises. Historical understandings also provide a context for considering the implications of unprecedented developments, such as global warming, upon future societies.

2

The Origins of Capitalism

How do historical sociologists examine evidence, make use of case studies and of cross-national and cross-temporal comparisons, construct arguments, and debate with one another? Let's try to answer that question by examining the debate over the problem that launched sociology: the origins of capitalism. This "debate" actually consists of a number of interweaving debates, distinguished by the different ways in which participants define capitalism. For Marx, capitalism is a relationship of exploitation, a system based on the assertion by capitalists of exclusive property rights over what once were means of production that were collectively owned or divided among various groups with partial and overlapping rights to work or collect part of what was produced. For Weber, capitalism was merely one species of systematic rational action. Marxist scholars have divided over whether capitalism is defined by production for a market or by the employment of wage labor. Weber's precise concern with the origins of just the first instances of rational action was replaced in the 1960s and 1970s by modernization theory, which found among people in many times and places an urge for unprecedented material plenty and a willingness to transform their societies in whatever ways were necessary to imitate modern peoples elsewhere. Yet other scholars characterize capitalism as a global system and see as their task tracing and explaining the globalization of local societies and economies.

If capitalism can be defined in so many different ways, then scholars can find its origins in many places and times and through many causal sequences. How, then, can we conduct research, critique past theories, and make intellectual progress? Is it possible to speak across those different debates? As we will see in later chapters, similar problems of competing definitions and overlapping debates that don't really engage with one another and reach conclusions also plague work on revolutions, states and social welfare policies, gender and the family – indeed, almost any topic.

Nevertheless, historical sociologists have found ways to cut through inconclusive debates. They have done so by focusing on identifying the moment of historical change. Once we know exactly when a significant change took place – what Sewell (1996) and Abrams (1982), whom we met in the previous chapter, call events – we then can ask what happened right before that moment and thereby find causes and identity sequences of contingent change. Let's see how this has been done with the origins of capitalism.

Weber has the virtue of being very clear on when he believes capitalism began. Weber saw feudalism as a "chronic condition" ([1922] 1978, p. 1086), incapable of being transformed through its own internal dynamics. As a result, he looked to an external force, the Protestant Reformation, to disrupt social relations and spark rational action and capitalism ([1916–17] 1958). While Weber's argument is theoretically elegant, it is factually wrong. Weber and historically ignorant sociologists who read him uncritically are unaware that earlier theologians offered critiques of medieval Catholicism similar to those of Luther and Calvin, or that English Protestantism gave rise to a libertarian communism as well as to a politically repressive and capitalist ideology (Hill 1972), or that Catholic theologians and officials quickly developed doctrines that blessed capitalist practices and rational action (Delumeau [1971] 1977).

The Protestant Reformation certainly was an event (in the sense that we use that word in this book), in that it disrupted and transformed everyday practices and social relations; however, to make his argument, Weber ignores other events that historians find were even more consequential for the outcomes that he seeks to explain. Although theory construction and the formulation of explanations for complex historical changes require decisions about which historical events matter, when simplification is taken too far it leads, as with Weber's *Protestant Ethic*, to distortion. Weber himself, in his final work, the *General Economic History*, acknowledges that capitalism had multiple, intersecting causes, many of which emerged long before Protestantism (Collins 1980). However, this late theory, with its very long time horizons, is unable either to explain why capitalism emerged at a particular moment or to account for its very uneven development in different regions of the "West."

Weberians and Marxists have built upon or compensated for Weber and Marx's shortcomings in different ways, creating traditions of theory building and research that have yielded particular insights or led to dead ends. Weber's Protestant Ethic thesis gave rise to modernization theory, an effort to broaden his argument about a transformation in a single time and place into "the search for equivalents of the Protestant ethic in non-Western societies" (Eisenstadt 1968, p. 17). Modernization theorists divide societies into traditional (where there is little social change because people are unable to imagine how they could better their material condition and therefore do not attempt to rethink or challenge the practices and beliefs they inherited from their ancestors) and modern. Modern societies are marked by a general "interest in material improvement" (Levy 1966, p. 746). Once, thanks to the Protestant Ethic, Europeans demonstrated that such improvement could be achieved through rational action, people "will always seek to implement that interest if the opportunity seems afforded" (ibid.). The task for modernization theorists, then, became figuring out what obstacles had to be overcome to achieve the economic growth and social transformation needed to become a modern society (Levy 1972).

There is very little contingency in modernization theory. Events are noticed mainly when they contribute to overcoming obstacles and fostering modernization. This theory does not seek to explain variation, since the end result – a desire for continual material improvement and the capacity to achieve that desire – is assumed to be or eventually to become the same everywhere. Lack of modernization, or slow growth, is explained as failure to reform traditional societies – failure that can be overcome anytime the people (or leaders, or outside aid givers) decide to follow the steps taken by successful modernizers. Modernization theorists have almost nothing to say about conflicting interests or exploitation, largely because they believe everyone benefits from modernity.

Several recent works address Weber's concerns with the role of religion in historical change with careful historical research and rigorous analysis. Mary Fulbrook (1983) offers an explanation for the diversity of Protestant ideologies that Weber ignored. She finds English Puritans and German Pietists adapted their purely theological doctrines to address economics and politics only when, and to the extent that, rulers challenged their institutional freedoms. Philip Gorski (2003) focuses Weber's theory in a different way, finding that Calvinism was most effective in unleashing a desire for discipline in the faithful themselves, and more vitally by the faithful as government officials and employers over their subjects and employees. It is not that Calvinism created capitalism or states, in Gorski's model; rather Calvinism made states more effective and ambitious. Gorski acknowledges that other Protestant denominations and Catholicism also fostered somewhat different and often lesser disciplinary impulses, and he is careful not to assert that the linkages between Protestantism and the disciplinary state affected other realms of human action as well, as Weber claimed. Similarly, Eiko Ikegami (1995) traces how Japanese religion and samurai notions of honor were transformed as the samurai were incorporated into the developing Japanese state (and later into capitalist enterprises as well). Ikegami is not claiming that Japan had a functional equivalent of Protestantism; instead she is pinpointing how Japanese religion shaped specific forms of Japanese enterprise and administration.

Fulbrook, Gorski, and Ikegami are careful first to specify what behaviors and institutions were affected by the new religious doctrines and then to delineate what affect those behaviors and institutions had on states or capitalism. They show how change can be confined to certain aspects of human action and don't assume that ideological or institutional change unleashes an all-encompassing rationality or modernity. Gorski, Fulbrook, and Ikegami, in being so careful, shy away from offering a general theory of the origins of capitalism. Fortunately, that remained the goal of Marxist histories.

Marx was interested in the origins of capitalism mainly to demonstrate that capitalists' property rights were illegitimate, rather than to specify when capitalism began or to detail the causal pathway from early to mature capitalism. Marx indicted early capitalists, first, for using force and fraud to convert collective feudal land rights into their private property and, second, for conquering non-European peoples:

> The discovery of gold and silver in America, the extirpation, enslavement and entombment in mines of the aboriginal population, the beginning of the conquest and looting of the East Indies, the turning of Africa into a warren for the commercial hunting of black-skins, signalised the rosy dawn of the era of capitalist production. These idyllic proceedings are the chief momenta of primitive accumulation. (Marx [1867] 1967, vol. 1, p. 751)[4]

Ultimately, Marx's history is about how capitalism and capitalists operate, not about their origins. As a result, Marx never pinpoints when capitalism began, nor does he answer the crucial question of why social actors were able to engage in primitive accumulation, and thereby launch capitalism, at a particular time but not earlier, and in Europe but not elsewhere.

Marx's vagueness about the timing of the beginning of capitalism and his lack of attention to how early capitalism differed from its mature form (which is what he was most interested in examining) left little guidance for the Marxists who, beginning in the 1940s, engaged in a debate on "the transition from feudalism to capitalism." These Marxists, regardless of their differences, agreed that their task was to explain how capitalism developed out of an existing social system. This might seem like a minor accomplishment: after all, all social systems and all social events are formed in whatever society existed before that moment of transition. However, many (perhaps most) social scientists are so eager to describe and analyze the event or social system they want to explain that they lose sight of the historical context in which it occurred. This certainly is a problem, as we saw above, with Weber and most Weberians, who, convinced that feudalism or traditional society was stagnant, ignore pre-capitalist dynamics and instead construct theories of how Protestantism or modernization abruptly created an entirely new social world.

Marxists took a very different approach from Weberians. Instead of identifying a single path from multiple, though vaguely described, traditional societies to capitalism or modernization, Marxists have drilled down into the historical evidence to try to pinpoint the time and place where capitalism began. In essence, Weberians (except for exemplars of careful history such as Fulbrook, Gorski, and Ikegami) became less historical than Weber, while Marxists became more historical than Marx.

Marxists, in their debates on the transition from feudalism to capitalism, disagreed on what capitalism was, and therefore on what signs of its origins they needed to identify. One position, first formulated by Paul Sweezy ([1950] 1976), defined capitalism as production for the market. These Marxists were, in a sense, like Weber. They did not see how feudal class relations could generate capitalism. Instead, they saw cities, which they believed existed in a sector outside of feudal society, as the source of markets and of a bourgeoisie.

The difficulty with this perspective is that there were extensive markets in feudal Europe, as well as in other pre-capitalist societies (including ancient Rome). However, the areas with the most extensive markets in medieval and Renaissance Europe, such as urbanized Italy, did not become the loci of subsequent economic development, despite their advantages of greater capital accumulation and their control over existing trade networks. The attempt to find the engine of capitalist transition outside of feudalism was as much of a dead end for Marxists as it was for Weber and modernization theorists.

Far more fruitful was the approach taken by Maurice Dobb (1947), whom Sweezy's argument was written to challenge. Dobb, following Marx more closely, defined capitalism as a relationship of exploitation. Dobb and his intellectual allies[5] looked for evidence of when and where peasants were dispossessed from the land and turned into wage laborers as landlords gained full control over land as private property. The advantage of this approach is that it focused analysis on an existing social system and asked what was the dynamic within feudalism that transformed it and in such a way as ultimately to yield capitalism.

The key historical moment for this school of Marxists was the Black Death of 1348, which is seen by most historians as the great divide in the history of feudal agrarian economies. The drastic decline in population made peasant labor scarce and ended the shortage of arable land. Peasants tried to renegotiate the terms of their tenancies or escape to where landlords offered better deals, while landlords sought to compel tenants to remain on their estates. Landlords succeeded in re-enserfing most of their tenants in Eastern Europe, while most English and French tenants won greater degrees of autonomy from their manor lords.

Is this the moment when capitalism began, the Marxist counterpoint to Weber's Reformation? Not quite. Maurice Dobb (1947) contends that English peasants used their new freedoms, and landlords adapted to their lesser control over tenants, by creating a "petty mode of production" characterized by the commercial leasing of land and limited proletarianization. He argues that full-fledged capitalism awaited the destruction of guild and aristocratic power in the 1640 English Revolution.

Dobb's analysis of the transition from feudalism to capitalism suffers from two major flaws. First, he is unable to explain why there was a lag of two to three centuries between the abolition of servile labor after the Black Death and the development of private property in land and the proletarianization of a plurality of peasants in the century following the Henrician Reformation (Lachmann 1987, p. 17). Second, he is unable to explain why similar petty modes of production, and similar late feudal political systems, produced a bourgeois revolution in England a century and a half earlier than in France. Dobb fails, on this second count, because he never identifies a dynamic internal to the petty (or feudal) mode of production that generated an English bourgeoisie capable of defeating the aristocracy in 1640 while stunting the growth of a similar class in France. While he never specifies the actual sequence of contingent events that led from the Black Death to English capitalism, he did focus research on the three centuries from the 1348 Black Death to the 1640 English Revolution, stimulating further debate and paving the way for further comparative historical research on class conflict and economic and political change in Europe.

The next major advances came from Robert Brenner (1976, 1982) and Perry Anderson (1974). Brenner and Anderson, like Dobb, saw the Black Death as a crucial turning point but analyzed its effects differently. Unlike Dobb, who focused almost exclusively on Britain, Brenner and Anderson compared Eastern and Western Europe and Britain and France. Brenner drew attention to communal village institutions, which he argued determined peasants' capacity to resist landlord demands in the aftermath of the Black Death. Peasant strength, or weakness, in turn affected "ruling-class self-organization" (Brenner 1982, p. 69) – i.e., the form of the state and the degree of merchant autonomy. Thus, in Eastern Europe where peasant communal organization was weak, landlords were able to force peasants into serfdom, but at the cost of economic stagnation and backwardness.

Anderson's picture of Eastern Europe is similar to Brenner's, but his causal sequence differs in one crucial respect. Anderson begins with the fact that Eastern European landlords were disorganized and isolated before the Black Death, which made them vulnerable both to foreign armies and to the armies of powerful nobles within their own countries. As a result, Eastern nobles were incorporated within powerful absolutist states. Those states had the capacity to suppress autonomous towns and re-enserf peasants and so better safeguarded the aristocracy's collective class interest than the more fragmented and decentralized states in Western Europe. Brenner and Anderson both look to changes in agrarian production to explain the organizational power of states, peasants, and merchants. For Anderson, ruling-class organization shaped peasant class capacity, while for Brenner the causality runs the other way.

Anderson's emphasis on the internal dynamic of the ruling class in *Lineages of the Absolutist State* allows him to show, in a more convincing way than either Dobb or Brenner, how feudalism was transformed into capitalism in Western Europe in the centuries after the Black Death. Remember Dobb merely said that the petty mode of production became capitalism after the destruction of the aristocracy, but offered no explanation for how the aristocracy was destroyed or where the bourgeoisie that destroyed the aristocracy came from. Brenner is best at explaining why Eastern Europe's economy remained backward, and also why France developed more slowly than England. Brenner contends that, in France, the aristocratic fraction with the greatest capacity to pursue its interests, the clique located within the state, appropriated revenues in ways that retarded the development of the forces of production. The high rate of extraction forced French peasants to have large families, subdivide their holdings, and engage in labor-intensive farming. The surplus extracted by the state-based aristocrats was spent on political investment, perpetuating feudal relations of production. Anderson argues that absolutist states, even as they perpetuated feudalism in the East, transformed the class dynamic in Western Europe by fostering autonomous towns, encouraging manufacture (initially for their armed forces), protecting foreign trade, and creating state offices and state debt. In Anderson's view, townspeople, manufacturers, traders, state bureaucrats, and state debt holders became the nucleus of a bourgeoisie. Anderson advances his analysis through comparisons between five Western and four Eastern European countries, as well as with the Islamic world and Japan. This gives him more leverage to identify significant variables and different causal paths than Brenner achieves by comparing East and West, and then France and England, or than Dobb, who only looks at England.

Anderson identifies a five-step causal sequence that brought Europe (or initially Britain) from feudalism to capitalism.

1   Landlord–peasant class conflict after the Black Death forced a reorganization of the aristocracy.
2   Politico-legal coercion was displaced upward into absolutist states.
3   The different forms of those states in Eastern and Western Europe were determined by three factors: the extent to which aristocrats were organized into estates, the degree

of urban autonomy, and the strength of foreign military threats.

4 The form of each state determined the degree and extent to which a bourgeois class developed under and subordinate to absolutism.

5 The bourgeoisie overthrew the absolutist states in Western Europe, making possible the unfettered development of capitalism.

This is a significant advance over all previous Marxist, and indeed non-Marxist, analyses of feudal dynamics and the origins of capitalism. Yet, problems remain with Anderson's analysis. He never actually analyzes the English Revolution. Although the French state was stronger, and cities and state officials were more powerful there, France's revolution came more than a century after Britain's, while Anderson's model would predict that the French state should have fostered a larger and more assertive bourgeoisie than its weaker English counterpart.

Neither Brenner nor Anderson is able to explain how, in the absence of a strong state in England, peasants who had been able to withstand aristocratic demands after the Black Death succumbed to landlord pressures two centuries later. Instead, Brenner merely asserts that English landlords became capitalists: "Lacking the ability to reimpose some system of extra-economic levy on the peasantry, the lords were obligated to use their remaining feudal powers to further what in the end turned out to be capitalist development" (1982, p. 84). What precisely those powers were beyond "their continuing control over the land" (ibid.), or how landlords used such control, Brenner never says. Similarly, Anderson never explains how the English Revolution transformed the absolutist state or fostered capitalism. (Such an analysis was left for a promised but never written sequel to *Lineages*.) Instead, he abruptly concludes his chapter on England: "Before it could reach the age of maturity, English absolutism was cut off by a bourgeois revolution" (1974, p. 142).

Anderson's causal analysis is weakest where, not surprisingly, his methodological vagueness is greatest – in the specification of agents. *Lineages* highlights broad categories of actors – aristocrats, peasants, bourgeois – all defined in

Marxian terms. Anderson's theoretically derived comparisons work well enough for Eastern Europe, where aristocratic agency was organized almost entirely through estates, and where almost all bourgeois were holders of state-granted urban privileges. His categories are sufficiently precise to analyze landlord–peasant conflict in Western Europe through the first three steps of his causal argument.

Anderson's inattention to the specification of agents becomes most problematic at the climax of his argument, in steps 4 and 5, when he seeks to explain how a bourgeoisie with interests opposed to the aristocracy developed within absolutism and why that bourgeoisie became revolutionary in its opposition to the ruling aristocratic class. Anderson never offers a methodology for identifying the new bourgeois. The sites of bourgeois class formation he identifies – state offices, autonomous towns, manufacture, and foreign trade – also were inhabited by aristocrats. How can we impute different class identities to occupants of the same sites? What factors allow us to know when actors realign their interests away from those of the absolutist states that once privileged them?

Anderson never answers those questions explicitly. When he writes of feudal power being redeployed within states, he opens up the possibility that power within feudalism can be lodged in, and exercised through, various institutional mechanisms. Clergies, provincial blocs of nobles, estates, corps of officeholders, chartered merchants, and monarchs and their retainers all thrived through the exploitation of feudal peasantries. They all were part of a feudal ruling class. Yet, as Anderson shows in his sequential narratives of cases, the forms of domination and exploitation can change. Because each type of feudal privilege is institutionally grounded, and not always through manors, it becomes possible to visualize the inhabitants of each type of absolutist institution as an elite, as I did in my own analysis of the origins of capitalism (Lachmann 2000).

Conflicts among elites can be understood as a distinct dynamic, operating prior to and alongside feudal class conflicts and international warfare as a contingent cause of structural change. Elites became bourgeois at the end of long chains of contingent conflict. Capitalist interests and class relations emerged as solutions to the double-barreled problems of feudal elite and class conflict within absolutist states. Thus, England had its bourgeois revolution a century and a half before France, and it quickly overtook the Netherlands and other Western European commercial centers to become the first industrial power, because elite conflict concentrated control over land and over local government in the hands of a gentry elite that had the organizational capacity and political leverage to guard its structural position against state elites from above and peasants and proletarians from below. The English gentry, in their efforts to defeat rivals in elite conflicts, managed to accumulate capital, proletarianize the labor force, and form a state best suited to protecting the domestic economy while conquering foreign markets. It was in this way that feudal elite and class conflicts led, through a series of contingent events, to an English state and agrarian mode of production that provided the preconditions for Britain's first making of industrial capitalism.

Our understanding of the origins of capitalism does not in itself explain either the subsequent contours of capitalist growth and industrialization or the emergence of a capitalist world economy. Yet, the methodological lessons we can draw from the above review of the debates over, and growing understanding of, the origins of capitalism can help us adjudicate among scholars who address economic development and the changing hierarchy of capitalist economies in later centuries. If we want to understand why certain countries became wealthier than others, and managed to exploit other regions of the world, we again need to follow the methods that produced greater understanding of capitalism's origins. Above all, we need to identify sequences of events that produced structural change.

Much work on economic development, especially that produced by economists, builds on the same assumptions that guide modernization theory (indeed, the bulk of development economists were schooled in modernization theory or utilize formal models that derive from that perspective). This approach assumes that historical period and temporal sequence don't matter, that development and economic growth can begin at any time.

This view has been challenged most powerfully by world systems theory. Developed by Immanuel Wallerstein (1974–2011) and Giovanni Arrighi (1994), world systems theory shows how each nation's economy became part of a global capitalist system that first emerged in the sixteenth century. Wallerstein demonstrates the effects of that system through careful comparisons of economies over time as they were drawn into the world economy. Both authors show, again through comparisons over time and across space, how countries at the core, semi-periphery, and periphery of the world system develop in very different ways, depending on whether and how they are exploited by or benefit from their position in the world economy. In essence, Wallenstein and Arrighi have written a series of contingent histories of different national, regional, and positional participants in the world economy, while drawing those elements together to show the structural dynamics of the entire world system itself.

Wallerstein and Arrighi, like all analysts, made choices of what elements to emphasize, and what paths of contingency to trace, in the world histories they have written. The coherence, and explanatory power, of their analyses come from their focus on the operation of the entire world system, and therefore they highlight the ways in which class and national actors are constrained by their positions in that system. Their model is less able explain why some countries shift position in the world system, and instead focuses on drawing out the implications of such shifts (for example, by South Korea from periphery to semi-periphery) for the countries' subsequent political structure and economic development.

Zeitlin (1984) addresses this lacuna in world systems theory through a single case study of Chile, showing that, thanks to its large reserves of key minerals, Chile had a path to becoming an industrialized core economy. The state could have built infrastructure, above all rail lines, and offered other subsidies to allow Chilean firms to develop independently of British mining interests. A domestic mining industry then would have created enough demand to stimulate a manufacturing sector. Owners of the large Central Valley estates managed to block such policies because they would have been taxed to support industrial development and because a growing industrial sector would have drawn workers away from agriculture, raising labor costs. Chile's fate was sealed in two civil wars in the 1850s and 1890s, which were won by the faction headed by large landlords, in part because the mining elite was divided on regional and familial lines. In the second civil war, the mining bourgeoisie was allied with an authoritarian president, so, ironically, the agrarian elite's victory also fortified electoral democracy even as it ensured Chile's dependent economic position. Zeitlin concludes, "class relations within nations shape the global relations between them" (1984, p. 234).

Zeitlin's critique of world systems theory reinforces the importance of contingency. While countries, and class and elite actors, are powerfully constrained by their position in the world system, openings for actions that transform social structure do emerge at times. Through carefully comparative analysis, or by tracing chains of contingency within single cases, it is possible to identify such moments of possibility. Yet, often, perhaps usually, such possibilities are not realized. As Zeitlin shows, Chile's self-serving elites managed to adopt policies that relegated their nation to the periphery and most of their fellow Chileans – though not themselves – to poverty.

The possibility of capitalist development also was undermined, in a series of contingent steps, in Renaissance Italy. Italian city-states were centers of long-distance trade, manufacture, and banking, yet reverted to feudal forms of agriculture and politics. Emigh (2009, whom we will examine in chapter 6), Aymard (1982), Epstein (1991), Tarrow (2004), and Lachmann (2000, ch. 3) offer differing though largely complementary analyses. What they share is a focus on a single negative case: Renaissance Italian city-states possessed some of the characteristics other authors identify as preconditions or causes of capitalism, yet capitalism did not develop there. This negative outcome leads these scholars to identify other factors or contingent sequences which created political and economic structures that differed both from feudal societies and from those places that in later centuries did develop capitalism. In so doing, these authors show that the particular ways in which cities exploited the countryside (analyzed differently by Aymard, Epstein, and Emigh) sapped innovation and investment in agriculture, and that elite and class conflict affected the institutional structure of city-states in ways that stymied the expansion of state capacities needed for capitalist development (Tarrow) and led elites to refeudalize the economy and polity (Lachmann).

Case studies, negative case studies, and cross-national and cross-temporal comparisons each are appropriate for answering particular questions. The task for historical sociologists is to identify the appropriate cases and to select the mode of analysis that will best allow them to build on and critique past contributions to ongoing debates or to open new problems for study. Taken together, the authors we have considered in this chapter contribute both to understanding the origins of capitalism and to illuminating the interactions between structure and contingent change. The analysis of structure and contingent change provides the historical context to understand agency, the topic of the next chapter.

3
Revolutions and Social Movements

Some events are more consequential than others. Revolutions are among the most momentous in world history. How can we study such epochal historical moments? How do we explain why social actors decide to take great risks to challenge the powerful at some rare times, when for the most part people resign themselves to the existing social order? As we see how some historical sociologists have sought to answer these questions, we will be able to explore methods for addressing the role of human agency in historical change.

Most people through most of human history have been poor, miserable, and exploited, and they have been unhappy about their condition. Misery is not enough to create a social movement or to spark a revolution. As Barrington Moore (1978, p. 161) puts it, "in the human repertoire of responses to deprivation and injustice an aggressive counterattack is scarcely the one to anticipate as automatic and somehow 'natural.'" If we want to explain why revolutions and social movements occur and how they matter, we need to work our way through three distinct steps.

- *First*, we must identify moments when revolutions or social movements occurred. This is partly a problem of definition, just as it is with explaining the origins of capitalism. As with the origins of capitalism, we can cut through inconclusive debates by focusing on identifying moments of historical change. In the case of revolutions, we need to find occasions when not just rulers were overthrown but the form of rule itself was transformed. In the case of social movements, we need to find moments when popular groups went beyond making demands and protesting and actually won significant concessions from those against whom they mobilized.

- *Second*, we need to examine how such moments of effective action against rulers differed from what came before. In other words, we need to explain why a revolution happened at one point in time and not earlier, or why a social movement won concessions at a certain moment and not before.

- *Third*, we need to specify how revolutions or successful social movements matter. It is not enough to list the concessions won or to enumerate those overthrown, dispossessed, exiled, or killed in a revolution. Rather, we need to compare the pre- and post-revolutionary states or social systems, or to specify how the concessions won by a social movement changed politics or social relations.

Let us examine the works of historical sociologists and historians who have been successful at carrying out each of these steps. It is unusual for a single study to succeed in all three tasks, although the first two steps are tightly linked in the most effective studies, and therefore we will discuss them together, since once a scholar identifies the moment of revolution that in turn focuses their search for causes. Conversely, some authors begin with an analysis of causes, and that then delineates the time span of revolution, although, as we will see, those who begin with the second step and work their way back to the first step end up with sloppier and less convincing analyses. Some insights come from scholars of revolutions, others from students of social movements; indeed, the two literatures overlap so much that we will do better if we consider both as part of a single discipline of popular mobilization and structural change.

Not surprisingly, many of those who study revolutions, and especially those who study social movements, do so because they are sympathetic to the movements' goals. Social movements, thus, spur academic study and also can create or reshape academic disciplines. The feminist movement led to the creation of gender or women's studies departments and programs in many countries, and made gender integral to history and sociology departments as well. Most US black studies programs were created in the 1960s and 1970s, at the height or in the immediate aftermath of the Civil Rights and Black Power movements. Today, universities in many countries have gender or women's studies departments or programs, and most US colleges and universities also have black or African-American studies programs. Other ethnic studies departments are most often located at US universities in cities or states with substantial populations of the groups that are the subjects of study. For example, Latino studies programs are concentrated in states with substantial Latino populations. For the most part, these programs were created at moments of heightened mobilization; indeed, they often were created in response to mobilizations on campuses that included, among other demands, the creation of women's or ethnic studies programs.

Movements demanding gender or racial and ethnic rights and recognition, and the academic programs they created, have had an affect on the broader field of sociology and on other academic disciplines as well. "Race, class, and gender" are seen, by many sociologists, as central, often the central, theoretical concepts and categories of their work, even when their work in fact is organized around other concepts and theories. Yet even when "race, class, and gender" is mainly an invocation of goodwill and inclusiveness (the sociological equivalent of the Father, the Son, and the Holy Ghost), it denotes sensitivity to groups and issues previously unrecognized and unstudied.

Area studies departments and programs have a more complex history. In the US, most began during the Cold War, with funding from the federal government, to train diplomats and spies to represent American interests around the world and to conduct research that would make US counter-insurgency strategies more effective – i.e., to help the US military and the CIA identify and kill insurgents in Latin America, Southeast Asia, and Africa (Wakin 1998). These departments were the intellectual successors to the anthropology and area or colonial studies programs in European universities, which developed out of a desire to understand and more easily rule the peoples of their non-European empires (Steinmetz 2012, 2007).

The wave of anti-colonial movements that won independence for most of the Third World in the decades immediately following World War II challenged the ways in which academic disciplines, including sociology, thought about and studied the non-Western world. The notion that Western scholars had biases that shaped (or distorted) their understandings and theories became integral to much work done in and about the global South. Some Western academics joined their Third World counterparts in acknowledging that such cultural biases and blind spots affected their work on their own countries as well. In recent decades, area studies programs have become centers for scholarship that is much more critical of Western imperialism and that challenges Western intellectual hegemony (although some have cashed in on the "War on Terror" funding bonanza to offer advice once again to the US military on how to be more effective at counter-insurgency). Today, area studies scholars raise pointed questions about whether theories developed to explain Western revolutions and social movements are useful for understanding Third World politics. I will try to address those concerns in this chapter by specifying the extent to which explanations of revolutions or social movements in one part of the world can be generalized.

Revolutions: Defining and Timing

Numerous scholars have offered a variety of definitions of revolutions.[6] As Goodwin (2001, pp. 8–9) reminds us, "Concepts as such are not more or less true, but more or less useful for generating falsifiable explanations of interesting phenomena." Nevertheless, when it comes time to list examples of revolutions and to specify the consequences of those revolutions, scholars' lists and hierarchies are remarkably similar. Theda Skocpol, whose book *States and Social Revolutions* (1979) is the most influential sociological analysis of revolutions yet written, sums it up best when she distinguishes among "social revolutions," which combine "the coincidence of societal structural change with class upheaval; and the coincidence of political with social transformation," from "political revolutions," which "transform state structures but not social structures, and . . . are not necessarily accomplished through class conflict," and rebellions, in which subordinate classes revolt, but "even when successful . . . do not eventuate in structural change" (p. 4).

All three of Skocpol's categories occur in relatively short time spans, a few years at most. Social movements, in contrast, can last for many years and, especially in the cultural realm, can affect social structure gradually. Yet, even such movements have their greatest impacts in much more concentrated periods of time, and, as we will see, the dynamic of social movements and the ways in which they interact with power holders is very different in moments where they are most consequential than during the long grinding years of relatively uneventful mobilization.

Let's see how Skocpol (1979) and Jeffrey Goodwin (2001) identify the timing of revolutions and then compare that with how Charles Tilly (1986, 1995) and Roberto Franzosi (1995) conceptualize the beginnings, middles, and ends of social movements and strikes. These four exemplars are very careful and precise in identifying the temporal boundaries of the phenomena they want to explain.

Skocpol sees revolution as a three-stage process. First, the old regime is fatally weakened by military defeat, which discredits the rulers and makes them appear vulnerable, and by a fiscal crisis, which angers both elites, who depend on the state for income, and the masses, who then face deprivation at the same time as the state attempts to tax them to realize new revenues. Skocpol finds that these events happened in the space of a few years: "1787–9 in France . . . the first half of 1917 in Russia, and . . . 1911–16 in China (1979, p. 47). Second, discontented elites and masses are able to disrupt the operation of the old regime and defy its officials with impunity. This happens over an even shorter period of time, mere months in 1789 France and 1917 Russia, and over a few years as communist challenges to the Kuomintang rolled across China from 1946 to 1949 (although in each Chinese province this period was brief until the communists inevitably gained control). Finally, the old regime crumbles and its leaders are killed or forced into exile. A revolution ends when a new regime has successfully asserted control over the territory once controlled by the old regime, which in France and Russia came after a few years of civil war, and in China far more rapidly, as the 1946–9 civil war (which defined the second stage of the Chinese Revolution) ended with the old regime's sudden collapse and flight to Taiwan.

Becker and Goldstone (2005) have compiled data on the "time from the collapse or overthrow of the old regime to the consolidation of a stable new regime . . . when it no longer faces internal elite or popular challenges that pose a significant threat to its existence" (pp. 184, 190). They find that major revolutions were consolidated in anything from less than a year (Iran in 1979) to four years (Russia after 1917), twenty-nine years (Mexico after 1910), thirty-one years (Vietnam after 1945), and thirty-eight years (China after 1911) (p. 190). Becker and Goldstone come up with much longer time spans than does Skocpol, partly because they date the start of some revolutions to the establishment of a moderate or coalitional new regime (as in Mexico in 1910, China in 1911, or Cuba in 1952) or consider the regime consolidated only when it finally ends attacks by a foreign power on its territory (as in Vietnam and Nicaragua), even though domestically the revolutionary regimes in both those countries consolidated their rule and carried forward radical reforms even as they were under foreign attack.

What makes Becker and Goldstone's article so valuable is that it brings together a great deal of data and is explicit and clear in its definitions and assumptions, so that "those who differ with our choices can then modify this table as they see fit and see if that affects our results" (2005, p. 190). As a result, we can clearly see that foreign powers can delay the consolidation of a revolutionary regime, or force it to compromise with opponents and create a government that institutes less significant reforms or no reforms at all, by intervening themselves or by funding and arming counter-revolutionary armies that usually are composed largely of mercenaries (as happened in most of the cases Becker and Goldstone list: France, Russia, Mexico, China, Vietnam, and Nicaragua, though not Iran, the fastest revolutionary regime to consolidate power). On Becker and Goldstone's much longer list of regime collapses, which include events Skocpol would define as political revolutions and rebellions along with social revolutions, the time span ranges from under a year to forty-two years.

Becker and Goldstone themselves have little to say about foreign intervention (they argue that foreign intervention consolidates domestic support for the new regime) and instead focus on the structure of the old regime and the extent to which the revolutionaries are able to (1) defeat old elites, (2) incorporate the civil service and military of the old regime into the new state, and (3) take advantage of already existing levels of human and cultural capital. The relative weight and causal effect of these factors cannot be settled in a single article, or in a few pages here. However, in specifying the timing of revolutions and the consolidation of new regimes, Becker and Goldstone have performed an essential first step, just as Skocpol did in distinguishing among three stages of revolution and clarifying the timing of each.

The Causes of Revolutions

What analytical leverage does Skocpol gain by focusing our attention on relatively brief periods when most of the revolutionary action took place, and by dividing the revolution into three stages? First, and most importantly, she is able to separate long and usually uneventful periods of mass misery and discontent from the much rarer and briefer periods of eventful action against ruling classes and regimes. There is a long tradition of historians and social scientists, echoed in much contemporary journalism and governmental analysis, who argued that revolutions came out of mass discontent or desperation.[7] The problem with that theory (which is so poorly specified that it is really just an assumption or assertion) is that, while there is lots of misery, there are few rebellions, and even fewer revolutions. The question then becomes, not why do people rebel, but why in a few instances do ruling regimes crumble in the face of rebellion?

We can best answer that question by focusing on the short periods when revolutions actually occur and then ask: What happened before then?

Scholars of revolutions have made their greatest contributions since the 1970s by shifting the question from what makes revolutionary movements strong to what makes regimes weak. Skocpol, as I noted above, argues that revolutions happen when states are weakened by defeat in foreign wars and by economic decline that produces a fiscal crisis within the state and sets elites against each other in a struggle to maintain their share of shrinking state revenues and of the overall economy. However, when Skocpol applies the model she developed to explain the three great social revolutions to the Iranian revolution she found a significant difference: "the Shah's army and police . . . were rendered ineffective in the revolutionary process between 1977 and early 1979 without the occurrence of a military defeat in foreign war and without pressures from abroad serving to undermine the Shah's regime or to provoke contradictory conflicts between the regime and the dominant classes" (1982, p. 267). Nevertheless, Skocpol was able to find a clear-cut starting point in 1975–7, when the Shah's regime was weakened by the decline of oil prices. Oil was the dominant sector of the Iranian economy and provided almost all state revenues. The ensuing fiscal crisis created mass discontent. The second phase began in 1977, when urban masses went into the streets to oppose the Shah's regime. The first phase can be timed by examining economic statistics and the second by looking at records of mass demonstrations. The third is dated by the moment when the Shah fled the country and the remaining elements of the old regime were unable to establish a new government, allowing a new regime to take and consolidate power.

Skocpol's finding, that in Iran a modern state could be weakened enough by economic rather than military forces to make possible a revolution, challenges her own conclusion in *States and Social Revolutions*, that "it seems highly unlikely that modern states could disintegrate as administrative-coercive organizations without destroying society at the same time, a modern social revolution would probably have to flow gradually, not cataclysmically, out of a long series of 'nonreformist reforms'" (1979, p. 293). Yet, while Skocpol did not anticipate either the Iranian and Nicaraguan revolutions of 1979 or those a decade later in Russia and Eastern Europe, her conceptual breakthroughs of focusing attention on the state as well as the revolutionaries and separating causes from consequences has made it possible for other scholars to analyze these recent revolutions. Some, like Goodwin (2001), have built upon her state-centered framework. Others identify different or additional causal factors.

Goldstone (1991) contends that "state breakdowns" occur when rapidly rising population creates heightened competition, especially among elites, for high-prestige jobs while also inducing inflation and a state fiscal crisis. Iran's rapid population growth in the 1960s and 1970s supports Goldstone's theory, which is not incompatible with Skocpol's arguments, but is less precise in being able to identify the brief moments when discontent (whether caused by demography, war, or economics) produces state breakdown and revolutionary action.

Charles Tilly (1993) seeks to explain "revolutionary situations," which he defines as the appearance of a credible contender to state power that enjoys support from a segment of the society, while the incumbent holder is unable to suppress the challenger. A "revolutionary outcome" is when the contender takes power away from the old ruler. Tilly is concerned with explaining when and why contenders are able to mount challenges and create revolutionary situations. He argues that contenders arise and win support when the incumbent regime makes new demands on its subjects (most often for higher taxes) that the ruler lacks the capacity to enforce. Tilly, thus, identifies regularities in the causes of revolutions across five hundred years of European history.

Tilly finds that the most successful states are able to demand steadily rising taxes, conscript subjects into the military, and win the loyalty of their citizens without provoking revolutionary challenges. Less successful states fail in those tasks and either accept low revenues and small armies (which renders them vulnerable to foreign invasion) or make demands that provoke revolutions. In some cases the post-revolutionary regimes are better able to collect taxes and draft soldiers (all three of Skocpol's social revolutions created much more powerful regimes than the ones they overthrew).

At other times, the new regime is just as weak as the old one, or even weaker, and so becomes a target for foreign attack or another revolution. Tilly's definition of revolution is much broader and more inclusive than Skocpol's. His model is best both for identifying factors that make certain states vulnerable to challenge and for explaining why those factors change over centuries as state capacities expand and the characteristics of the local communities, upon which states make demands and revolutionary movements compete for support, change. Tilly's model is not very helpful for explaining how post-revolutionary governments differ from the regimes they overthrew, a problem that Skocpol's model is much better able to address, as we will see in the last section of this chapter.

Why Revolutionaries Win, and Why They Lose

Skocpol and Tilly, through their focus on the state, make us realize that it is not enough to examine revolutionaries' motives or capacities. Revolutions, like wars and social movements, have at least two sides. If the incumbent power holders are strong and unified, they cannot be defeated. That is not a pleasant realization, but unfortunately it is true. Skocpol shows it in her comparison of three social revolutions. Tilly, whose model also is well suited for reaching this understanding, identifies the characteristics that make states invulnerable to revolution in particular eras. Goodwin (2001) shows it in his analysis of the numerous revolutionary movements in Central America, Southeast Asia, and Eastern Europe from 1945 to 1991.

Goodwin addresses a somewhat different problem than Skocpol. Instead of just focusing on successful social revolutions, Goodwin compares successful and unsuccessful revolutions and builds a causal explanation for their divergent outcomes. He also explains why revolutionary movements in El Salvador, Guatemala, and Peru were able to sustain armed rebellions for decades, even in the face of massive violent repression by the state. Thus, Goodwin, in addition to comparing revolutionary movements that prevailed or were defeated over relatively short time spans, compares movements that were quickly crushed and those that held out for decades before they were ultimately defeated or finally agreed to negotiated settlements that left the incumbent regimes and ruling classes with their power and privileges largely intact.

Like Skocpol, Goodwin sees revolutions as targeted against states, and therefore their fates are determined largely by the states' internal structure, capacities, and links to elites. Goodwin identifies different factors that weaken states and create openings for opposition than does Skocpol. He points to the disruptions of Japanese occupation and World War II in Southeast Asia, the key role of the US as the sponsor of both highly cyclical agro-export sectors and repressive military regimes in Central America, and Gorbachev's reforms and the sudden withdrawal of Soviet support for the Communist Party regimes in Eastern Europe.

Goodwin, thus, expands the analysis from Skocpol's model and identifies additional factors that determine if, when, and where revolutions occur. Most significantly, because of his focus on absent, failed, and stalemated revolutionary movements, he identifies multiple contingent paths and identifies the aspects of state organization and capacity, and of elite organization and class structure, that enhance or limit a movement's coherence and efficacy.

Goodwin's model differs from Skocpol's in large part because he is examining different sorts of societies. In all his cases, external powers matter and undermine regimes, even in the absence of the military defeats that were so central to the three social revolutions Skocpol analyzes. Since the states Goodwin studies all were dependent on great powers, their internal dynamics differed from the old regimes in France, Russia, and China. However, external geopolitical and economic forces matter in Goodwin's cases because of their effects on states, and on the elites that inhabited and fought for position within those states. Changes in state form and capacities and in elite structures, in turn, were decisive in creating openings for, or defeating, revolutionary movements.

Stasis, the absence of new external pressures or internal change, created durable repressive regimes in some countries, while in others a fatal combination of "armed forces of infrastructurally weak states that employed indiscriminate violence" (Goodwin 2001, p. 217) made it possible for revolutionary movements to continue to recruit followers willing to die in the hundreds of thousands over decades. The power of Goodwin's model comes not just from his Skocpolian focus on the state, but also because he is so careful at identifying moments when structural openings were created for revolutionary movements to take effective action that in rare cases achieved victories, more often led to defeat, and in others prolonged civil wars that were ultimately won by repressive states.

Similarly, Jeffery Paige (1975) finds that peasants were angry and challenged those who dominated them throughout the Third World from 1948 to 1970 (the years for which he collected data). In most newly independent countries, peasants and agrarian laborers were unsuccessful in altering exploitative land tenure arrangements and had to settle for what Paige labels "agrarian reform commodity movements" or "agrarian reform labor movements." In a few instances, peasants managed to mount "agrarian revolts . . . a short intense movement aimed at seizing land but lacking long-run political objectives," and, even when successful, peasants "once again relapse into political apathy" (1975, p. 43). Agrarian revolutions, which can be either socialist or nationalist, are exceedingly rare. While Paige's definition of revolution is somewhat different from that of Skocpol or Goodwin, he too sees the fundamental cause of revolution as a breakdown in the ruling regime (in his case, the key rulers are regional agrarian ruling classes, who are not necessarily a state elite or national ruling class).

Paige, by comparing agricultural export sectors, finds that only certain specific class and state structures can come apart in a way that makes possible an agrarian revolution. Also, like Skocpol and Goodwin, Paige sees a clear connection between the vulnerabilities of the old regime, the sort of revolt or revolution that develops out of those weaknesses and the new regime that is created by the revolt or revolution. Unlike Skocpol and Goodwin, Paige is less interested in geopolitical dynamics that might weaken states or agrarian ruling classes. He draws a direct line from the agrarian class system to revolution, although he allows that class relations in an agricultural region can be disrupted or transformed by external political events at the state level, by nearby mining or industrial sectors, or by ideologically (often religiously) motivated social movements. The great advantage of Paige's focus on agrarian export sectors is that it allows him to (1) explain why most post-1945 revolutions and rebellions have begun in those sectors of Third World countries, (2) find structural factors that can account for peasant revolutionary strength across countries, and (3) explain why some ruling classes succumbed to revolution while most did not.[8]

Peasants and other protesters are not fools; nor are they suicidal. They don't join fights they know they can't win. Revolutions begin when states show weakness and when ruling elites are divided. Sometimes revolutionaries miscalculate. Most often, that happens when elites appear weak at the local level and protesters, who lack access to information about the rest of their country, mistake local particularities for the general national condition. Hung (2011) finds this happened again and again as Chinese peasants in the eighteenth and early nineteenth centuries attacked landlords or tax collectors and then were crushed as provincial elites or the national government maintained their capacity to mobilize armed forces to fight localized rebellions. However, when in the early twentieth century the Chinese state was weakened and elites divided, peasants were able to bring down the regime. Hung, through his careful analysis of the dynamics of peasant protests and revolts, is able to show that factors that account for the former don't necessarily predict the latter. By distinguishing protests and revolution, he is able to identify the rare conditions under which protests escalated and amalgamated into revolts that culminated in the Taiping Rebellion and the two twentieth-century revolutions, while other protests resulted mainly in state repression combined occasionally with minor concessions.

Sixteenth- and seventeenth-century English peasants generally were more accurate in their opportunistic rebellions, targeting counties where elites were divided and rebelling at moments when local elites were in conflict with the crown. When peasants were off on their timing, acting on old news of local divisions or disputes with the king, their rebellions were easily crushed by county governments or with the aid of royal forces (Lachmann 2000, pp. 180–5; Charlesworth 1983).

We can see the state's importance, and the necessity of measuring the degree and dynamic of elite unity and relations, when we consider the limitations of one of the masterpieces of history: Georges Lefebvre's *The Great Fear of 1789* ([1932] 1973). The Great Fear was a crucial event in the French Revolution. Waves of rumors (mainly that nobles were conspiring against the king) spread across France. When those rumors arrived in a town or village, peasants responded by attacking, and sometimes massacring, local nobles and officials. This fatally weakened the royal state and led many nobles to flee the country. Lefebvre traces, perhaps better than any other historian, what actually happens in the second stage of a revolution, when rulers are challenged and attacked with impunity and the old regime crumbles.

Lefebvre, unfortunately, is piecemeal in his explanation of why peasants believed and acted on rumors of the plot against the king. He first mentions hunger and unemployment, and argues that they became worse in 1787–9. Then several chapters later he discusses the calling of the Estates General and how the election of delegates and the king's call for communities to write *cahiers de doléance* (petitions of grievances) led peasants to decide that their true opponents were the nobility and not the king. However, Lefebvre never relates the economic and political factors he discusses to each other, nor does he organize them into a causal argument. His narrative is compatible with Skocpol's argument that revolutions follow state breakdown and that state breakdown involves elite splits, and there is an implicit Goldstone-like argument that overpopulation fueled peasant anger. However, unlike Skocpol or Goldstone, Lefebvre is never explicit about how the elements of his story fit together into a causal argument. The causal, as opposed to narrative, coherence of his book comes from our reading of it in light of our knowledge of other revolutions and our ability retrospectively to read more recent theories onto the story Lefebvre tells.

The greatest problem with Lefebvre, and other empirically rich but theoretically thin narratives, is that the revolutionaries appear to be merely angry, and anger, no matter how compellingly conveyed, can't explain what sort of new regime the revolutionaries created. Indeed, the deeper historians go into the minds of ordinary revolutionaries, the more diverse their complaints and desires appear, and the harder it becomes to understand why some revolutionaries gained power and why the new regimes responded to some popular demands and not others. Just as a greater understanding of how miserable peasants or urban workers are will not help us explain when and where revolutions occur, so too greater knowledge of how the oppressed think will not explain the origins of revolutions, although, as we will see in the last part of this chapter, such cultural analysis is essential to understanding what sort of regime emerges at the end of a revolution.

What Are Social Movements, and When Do They Occur?

Social movements are much more drawn out, and occur much more frequently, than revolutions. Often multiple groups, and also disorganized masses, protest. Protesters at times give multiple and contradictory reasons for demonstrating or for acts of violence. With the help of historians, we often read coherence back upon confused actors and contradictory events. Protests are given names and distinct purposes retrospectively, through the words or writings of leaders, or in terms of what gains they ended up achieving. The US Civil Rights movement is understood, and its many diverse and often contradictory actors and disparate events are given coherence retrospectively, in terms of the words of its leaders (above all Martin Luther King, Jr.) and in terms of the legal and legislative victories it won for voting rights and to end Jim Crow. African Americans' economic agenda, which went largely unfulfilled, has received far less attention from historians and social scientists who examined that social movement. Similarly, anti-colonial movements had multifaceted agendas, but in most cases their main victory was the end of foreign rule, and the other demands made by those movements, or the reality that some movements demanded citizenship rights within their empires rather than independence, are slighted in historical studies. As a result, the crucial questions of why social movements achieve or are granted a few of their demands and not others, and who decides which demands should be met, are rarely answered by social movement scholars. We will see, in the rest of this chapter, how those questions can be answered by examining a few exemplary studies that place them front and center.

Charles Tilly examined protests over spans of centuries. He began by amassing data sets of protests and identifying periods, often lasting decades or centuries, of widespread protests. His next step was to distinguish among different types of protests. He asked who was protesting: Was it peasants, taxpayers, or urban workers? He also specified the reason for protests: Were tenants protesting the high rents demanded by landlords, or were the protesters taxpayers angered at high taxes? Once Tilly was able to collect and organize data on numerous protests, he was able to identify key transitions. His greatest finding, which he documented for both Britain (1995) and France (1986), was that the reasons for protests shifted from being about high rents and against landlords to being about high taxes and against government officials.

Tilly's model is based on the idea that protests and social movements are a response to the demands and capacities of the powerful and not an expression of generalized grievance. As the character, identity, and demands of the powerful change, so too do protests and protesters. Tilly's work is a huge advance over "relative deprivation theory,"[9] which, like the misery theory of revolutions, assumes that, if conditions get worse, people will protest. The problem with relative deprivation theory is that it lacks a historical basis.

In reality, those who are most deprived often are quiet. If we want to explain why the relatively privileged – for example, Chinese university students in 1989, or US, Mexican, and Western European students in the 1960s – were at the forefront of protest, we need to look less at changes in their conditions or in their perceptions of their conditions and focus instead on how state actions alter the overall structure of power in a society. Thus, Zhao (2001) finds that the mass student movement in China (probably the largest such movement in world history) found room to mobilize as a result of state reforms. The pre-1989 reforms did not liberalize political expression (as the massacre that ended the student occupation of Tiananmen made clear). Instead state reforms inadvertently heightened competition among student groups and sharpened the lines between protesters and state, provoking the protests. Yet, Zhao finds that, even in total defeat, the student movement had an effect by setting in motion a series of elite struggles that restructured power within the state. Protests, in China in the 1980s or in the US, Europe, or Mexico in the 1960s, can matter a great deal, even if the consequences are not at all what the protesters demanded or even what their opponents sought to achieve.

Protesters' identities, and therefore the ways in which they think about allies and enemies, are created historically, in a series of contingent interactions between popular groups and elites. That is why Tilly's work is so important: he shows how, when state elites gained power over landlords, the demands upon and identities of non-elites were transformed. That transformation changed protesters' understandings of who they were and of their interests and enemies. If we just look at how revolutionaries or protesters think and act, if our goal is to resurrect protesters' biographies in as much detail as possible, we can lose sight of the ways in which dialogue (which often occurs in violent actions rather than words) between protesters/revolutionaries and power holders transforms both sides.

Our ultimate goal is to explain how protests or revolutions matter, and to do that we need to construct theories of how structural change occurs. Protesters' thoughts and actions necessarily are part of that process and an element, often a major element, in theory, but they can't be studied alone. As Abrams (1982, p. 332) puts it so well,

> The real danger of resurrectionism [the effort to resurrect the thoughts and lives of protesters] is not that historians and sociologists will be seduced into mere impressionism and a mass flight from theory; it is that they will encourage the belief (among themselves or others) that the theoretical work necessary to know the past can be done adequately in the very act of representation; the belief that enough facts, or intimate enough facts, will of themselves show us the theoretical reality of capitalism or feudalism, the extended family or peasant society.

Let us see how two exemplary works of historical sociology construct causal models that can explain both the process of popular mobilization and the effects of such mobilization upon social structure.

Roberto Franzosi (1995) examines one of the most significant forms of social movements in the twentieth century: labor unions. His goal is to explain why strikes occurred when and where they did in Italy during the post-World War II decades. Franzosi combines quantitative and qualitative analysis. He first created a massive data set that included the basic facts on each strike: date, duration, location, union, employer, and outcome (i.e., whether the workers gained better wages, benefits, or working conditions). He also used newspaper accounts of the disputes to trace the dynamics of each labor dispute: what set it off, what tactics workers and employers used, and how those tactics changed in the course of the strike as each side responded to the other's tactics.

What is Franzosi able to explain with his data and analysis? First, he shows how workers and their unions respond to openings in national politics created by divisions among employers or between capitalists and state officials, and that many strikes are timed to influence bargaining over national labor contracts. He finds that union tactics and the dynamics of strikes differ depending on the goal and the degree of unity among bosses and the state. Finally, and most significantly, Franzosi shows that massive strike waves (above all the "hot autumn" of 1969) follow very different dynamics than the bulk of strikes, which are isolated and involve fewer workers. That is why models that crunch all the strike data together produce misleading results, since they meld together the different causal paths of normal strikes and strike waves.

Waves are produced partly by imitation and inspiration, as groups of protesters look to and learn from each other. But waves also reflect larger structural openings as well as cascading patterns of weaknesses among ruling groups. When rulers fail to quell a strike, riot, or protest, they then (in order to avoid appearing weak) overreact to further popular mobilizations in ways that strengthen mass outrage and resolve and can open splits among elites, which in turn further convinces protesters that this is the moment for effective action.

Piven and Cloward (1971) argue that waves of riots and demonstrations in the US during the 1930s and 1960s led to the establishment or expansion of social benefit programs for the poor (as we will discuss in more detail in chapter 5). Markoff (1996a) finds that democratization (which he defines as the grant of voting rights to all or a part of the population) happened in waves, in large part because rulers sought to pre-empt more radical demands at the end of the two world wars and during periods of working-class mobilization.

We can be aware that waves occur, and then find both the causes and consequences of waves, only by conducting large-scale comparative historical analysis or, as Franzosi or Piven and Cloward do, by tracing a single country over a long time span. Rich case studies of a single strike, protest, or reform are not capable of identifying if that single case is part of a wave, and therefore can't differentiate the special dynamics of waves from those of isolated protests.

Franzosi, Markoff, and Piven and Cloward each use historical evidence and construct their arguments about waves in different ways. Franzosi builds his analysis of strike waves on a foundation of detailed, micro-level evidence. He shows that Italian strike waves operate in particular ways that reflect the structure of unions and of firms in Italy and the ways in which the Italian state regulates and intervenes in strikes. This allows him to show that the wave itself alters those structures, and thus to specify the wave's full range of effects: not just upon what demands workers make and what gains they win, but upon the structure of employer–worker relations and the organization of unions and of the state, which together provide the context of future class relations. Thus, at the end of a strike wave, workers are not just better off materially, but their capacity to engage in strikes and strike waves in later years is enhanced or reduced.

While Franzosi's study is of a single country, he provides a methodological and theoretical basis for cross-country comparisons. For example, strike waves occurred in a very different structural context and had dramatically different consequences in the US: the wave of sit-down strikes in 1936–7 resulted in significant victories for American workers both in the workplace and in national politics, while the 1946 strike wave produced gains within firms but major political defeats at the national level. Franzosi's model could be used to explain those differences with Italy and over time in the US. This would allow for a more dynamic understanding of US politics than does Piven and Cloward's approach. They see protest waves as almost automatic reactions to poverty that operate in largely consistent ways on an unchanging US political structure, producing similar gains in the 1930s and 1960s. Conversely, Markoff is sensitive to changes in capitalism and world geopolitics over the course of the nineteenth and twentieth centuries. As a result, he is able to identify the different complexes of causes that came together in different eras to produce waves of demands for, and grants of, voting rights in particular regions of the world.

Franzosi and Markoff are much more precise than Piven and Cloward in identifying differences in social movements across time and place. Not all strikes or protests are the same. Waves may have similar structural characteristics, even as their causes and consequences differ greatly. The lesson is that grievances are not enough to produce protests, let alone waves of protests. Nor are demands directly translated into concessions. What social movements or revolutions are able to accomplish cannot be understood by looking at protesters' demands or even at their degree of cohesion and intensity. For example, McAdam (1990) offers a compelling account and explanation for civil rights protesters' willingness to risk their lives in the Mississippi Freedom Summer of 1964. When it comes time to discuss the consequences of Freedom Summer, McAdam speculates on how it inspired later demonstrators and the counterculture, but he does not attempt to connect the social movement to legislation or politics beyond the movement. Even if he wanted to do that, the evidence and arguments he develops in his book would not be of much help in that broader task. As a result, although McAdam takes us into the minds, actions, and organizational networks of protesters, we don't advance in trying to understand why some of the movement's demands were achieved while others were not.

Roger Gould (1995) takes a very different approach to studying social movement activists than does McAdam. Gould is trying to solve a puzzle: the "majority of the insurgents [in both 1848 and 1871] were indeed workers" (p. 4), but "these two Parisian revolutions began differently, ended differently, and were understood by their protagonists as thoroughly different kinds of struggles – or, to put the same point another way, they were struggles between protagonists who understood themselves differently" (p. 7). In other words, Gould is not just interested in explaining the level of commitment; he also wants to explain how protesters' goals, networks of alliance, and accomplishments were transformed over time.

Gould finds a complex and confused relation between grievance, identity, and action, "a multidimensional world of crossed purposes and digressions." Unlike McAdam, he discovers that it is necessary to look beyond protesters' grievances, solidarity, and intensity of commitment and examine structural changes in the state and the economy and in the spatial organization of Paris to understand how Parisian radicals saw themselves and their opponents and formulated their demands. Like Franzosi in his analysis of strike waves, Gould finds that the "major insurrections" of 1848 and 1871 had different dynamics from the years of non-revolutionary "collective struggles about wages, hours and control over shop-floor practices" (1995, p. 199).

What is most valuable about Gould's approach is that it is historical in the way he both poses questions and finds answers by looking at how social structure, and therefore antagonists' positions and understandings, changed over time. Social movements make demands against opponents, who themselves are embedded in a global, national, and local social structure. The methods that can understand cause and effect begin with the realization that protests are channeled within that social structure, and that the openings that social movements and revolutions create vary as the structure changes. It is their lack of attention to change over time that limits the explanatory power of Piven and Cloward's model and McAdam's ethnography. The effort to trace contingent change, and to locate the role of social movements in contingent chains, sets the research agenda for Tilly, Franzosi, and Gould and allows them to show when and how social movement participants are able to take effective action.

How Do Revolutions and Social Movements Change History?

I answered this question in part in the previous section as we discussed how strike waves, mass protests, and waves of democratization altered social structure. Skocpol makes an important conceptual advance when she separates her analysis of the causes of revolution from the outcomes. As you might anticipate from my discussion above of how she explains the origins of revolutions, Skocpol sees the consequences of revolutions largely in terms of the ways in which revolutionaries were able to enhance the power of the states they seized. What is crucial for her, and for any successful analysis, is to examine the revolution as a brief period of heightened contingency when actors are able quickly to transform social structures. Our job, as comparative historical sociologists, is to trace those contingent chains and to draw comparisons with other revolutions, strike waves, or social movements. That is how we can sharpen our explanations and build theories that can be applied beyond single cases.

Let me illustrate how we can trace and explain revolutionary contingency, and thus explain the consequences of revolution, by focusing on what is the single best sociological analysis of a revolution: John Markoff's *The Abolition of Feudalism* (1996).

Abolition is an enormous advance over previous works on revolutions in general and the French Revolution in particular. Coming to the most studied revolution, and probably the most studied historical event, in human history, Markoff makes significant additions to our understanding. His achievement is due, in part, to his dedication of decades of effort to create two massive data sets. One specifies the participants, targets, goals, and outcomes of each instance of rural insurrection during the Revolution (this is similar in scope and detail to Franzosi's data set on Italian strikes). A second data set of every complaint in the *cahiers de doléance* allows Markoff to get at the attitudes and cultures of nobles, clergy, and the Third Estate (whom he breaks down further with additional data on regional and class differences) in each locality in 1789 France.

Markoff uses the first data set to trace the dynamic of revolutionary action, a far more comprehensive version of what Lefebvre achieved for the Great Fear. The second data set allows him to show how French participants in the Revolution conceived their demands, thought about their actions, and understood and responded to their opponents. Together, Markoff's analysis of action and participants' perceptions of events and of their changing situation creates what he describes as a motion picture of social transformation. This yields three major insights.

First, popular social movements and revolutions may be built upon the miseries and grievances of the masses, but they are directed at targets based on the revolutionaries' careful study of divisions and weaknesses within the ruling forces. Markoff asks why seigneurs became the prime targets of peasants during the Revolution, and why the legislative abolition of feudalism was the greatest achievement of the Revolution. His answer is that conflicts among nobles and with the bourgeois of the Third Estate suggested to peasants that anti-seigneurial protests might bear fruit. The meetings at which the *cahiers* were composed gave peasants an unprecedented and unparalleled opportunity to hear the divisions within and between clerical, noble, and bourgeois estates, divisions that were sharpest over the issue of seigneurial privileges.

> It hardly seems surprising then, that the proportion of insurrections targeting the seigneurial regime now doubled in the spring [of 1789]. The country people were discovering that if they pushed hard there would be at least some support from significant portions of the Third Estate and an important portion of the clergy and they were probably aware of the divided and ineffective capacity of the nobility to defend themselves. (Markoff 1996b, p. 495)

Markoff's research confirms and deepens Skocpol's theoretical claim that revolutions proceed and succeed based on the extent to which revolutionaries can discover and exploit weaknesses among those who dominate the old polity or economy. Successful revolutionaries are skilled at reading and responding to elite divisions and weaknesses in the short term.

Second, rebels and defenders of old regimes each can misread social structure by seeing broad openings in unusual local conditions (we saw that in our discussion of protests and peasant rebellions above). However, in a full-fledged revolution, those readings and misreadings determine not just who wins and who loses but the substance of the changes achieved by the revolutionaries. The members of the National Assembly were wrong in thinking that the abolition of feudal privileges would quiet the masses, but that mistaken reading of popular opinion determined the ultimate legacy of the Revolution.

Third, the goals and achievements of a revolution can be altered in the course of events. Markoff's study of the *cahiers* demonstrates that the goals of the Third Estate varied within and across localities. Revolutionaries often had numerous grievances and desires for change. Decisions of which demands to press, and which to lay aside, changed as revolutionaries attempted to recruit allies and tested the strength of their opponents. Revolutionary programs may be written by intellectuals or leaders beforehand, but they are altered and partially realized in the process of revolution. Markoff inverts the conceptual structure of works such as Skocpol's *States and Social Revolutions*. Instead of finding causes and then comparing outcomes, while leaving the revolutions themselves as largely unstudied black boxes, he focuses on the complexity of the revolution itself. He finds the various causes in the different manifestations of revolution and explains the outcomes through the process of revolutionary parry and thrust across the broad and varied field of a France peopled by actors with differing local identities and complex social locations.

People have grievances and are moved to join others to address those grievances. However, once protests or revolutions begin, movements divide, allies are gained and lost, and opponents take actions that demand responses. The ultimate outcomes cannot be predicted or understood merely by finding the initial causes of the uprising. Markoff shows that it is possible for us as historical sociologists to gather the data and construct analyses to understand what happened and why. The sociology of revolutions is important in itself but also as a laboratory to construct more sophisticated methods for tracing and explaining contingency. Revolutions are fast-moving and confusing events, but the best works on revolution bring methodological and conceptual clarity to the study of social change.

4
Empires

For most of human history some peoples have been able to dominate others, either in formal empires or through indirect means. An empire, in Julian Go's (2011, p. 7) definition, is "a sociopolitical formation wherein a central political authority . . . exercises unequal influence and power over the political (and in effect sociopolitical) processes of a subordinate society, peoples, or space." This chapter does not offer a critical review of the myriad definitions of empire. Those definitions all agree that empires differ from non-imperial polities in that they exert power over territories and peoples beyond their core polity, and that the essential dynamic of an empire is produced by the interaction between the core's efforts to sustain or expand and deepen its rule over peripheries and the peripheries' efforts to weaken or end the core's rule over them. The imperial dynamic is a temporal dynamic, which means that both imperiums and subordinate territories can be understood only as changing products of past sequences of conquest, incorporation, and resistance.

A failure to see empires as dynamic and contingent social systems mars S. N. Eisenstadt's *The Political Systems of Empires*, a massive comparative study of ancient empires whose publication in 1963 helped revive interest in comparative historical sociology. Eisenstadt mined a vast array of historical cases to find what he saw as commonalities in the political organization of empires. His main finding is that imperial power in all empires depended on the creation of what he labels "free-floating resources" – i.e., resources not tied to local institutions, such as profits from long-distance trade or mining. The expansion or decline of such free-floating resources then becomes the main dynamic in Eisenstadt's history, although he mainly asserts rather than explains their ebb and flow. He pays little attention to how empires went about exploiting conquered territories and offers no explanation at all for how and why subject peoples sometimes rebelled. As a result, Eisenstadt's historical study is timeless: the empires he studies seem little constrained by their past histories, and their rise and decline are presented as consequences of ad hoc events.

Of course, the most consequential events for empires are their conquest of colonies, and for colonies it is their subordination within an empire. When we study imperial societies in isolation, as many sociologists and historians do, we lose sight of how such dominant societies benefit from and are shaped by their efforts to extract wealth and exert geopolitical control over other parts of the world. When we examine former colonies, and territories that were indirectly ruled, we need to pay attention to the ways in which they continue to be shaped and limited by the ways in which they were exploited in the past. Such past exploitation is compounded by, and makes more likely, present-day forms of domination.

Any examination of the US economy that fails to take into account that country's hegemonic position in the world economy will be partial and distorted. Any study of US politics that leaves out America's repeated interventions around the world will fail to understand how the federal government allocates its budget, how parties compete for power, how Americans think about themselves and their nation, and how the national government institutes and implements its civilian programs. Even when a country, like Britain or France, no longer retains its empire, its economy, culture, and political system, and the ethnic make-up of its population and the relations among groups in that society, can only be understood in terms of that colonial legacy.

How have historical sociologists tried to make sense of the ways in which imperialism and informal modes of domination have affected both the rulers and the ruled? One approach is to examine how colonialism has shaped national identities. In the introductory chapter, we saw Wallerstein's argument that India, as a cultural category and also as a political unit with set boundaries, was created by British conquest and by the independence movement. Had a French effort to conquer part of British India succeeded, India might be divided into northern and southern cultures and countries. Or had the independence movement united Hindu and Muslim activists, or if the last British overlords of India had pursued a different strategy, there might not have been a partition, and present-day India, Pakistan, and Bangladesh would be a single nation. For Wallerstein, national identities coincide with national borders, and both are determined in conflicts among imperial powers and then by the successes or limits of independence movements.

Benedict Anderson argues that imperial powers also created, partly by design and partly inadvertently, national cultures in their colonies through the imposition of their own languages (English, French, and Spanish) upon linguistically diverse populations. Newspapers, created partly by imperialists and partly by locals (in the latter case often to express resistance to foreign rule), fostered "print-languages" that began to supplant native oral languages and "laid the bases for national consciousness . . . the embryo of the nationally imagined community" ([1983] 1991, p. 44). Anderson identifies language and print culture as the causal hinge between imperial conquest and cultural domination and the emergence of nationalist resistance. For Anderson, culture matters most at a specific historical juncture, and its effect is mainly on nationalist feelings, which then have their own causal power. His model implies that, once national identities are created, culture then has a lesser influence, even though he does not trace that later history.[10]

Imperialism also affects social relations and ethnic identities and divisions within colonies. Pierre Bourdieu began his career in Algeria in the last years of French rule. He found that not only was Algerian identity, as both nationalist and Arab, formed in the struggle against French rule, but local identities also were transformed, resulting in the marginalization of non-Arabic speakers as members of tribes rather than as full-fledged Algerians (Bourdieu 1958).[11] Thus, French colonialism, in creating a particular sort of Algerian identity, limited the ability of the marginalized to enter into and benefit from the modern society and capitalist economy. Bourdieu's focus on culture and its place in social relations limits his attention to the development and operation of the Algerian economy and state. As a result, he has little to say about Algeria's post-independence trajectory or on the relationship between colonial and post-colonial institutions and politics.

It is not only the colonized but also the colonizers who are affected by imperialism. Kumar (2003) argues that contemporary British identity reflects its imperial past, that Britons think about what it means to be British and how their nation differs from others in terms of ideas and practices that were developed during the nineteenth century heyday of empire. His analysis is pitched at the cultural level; he is concerned mainly to explain, and he draws his evidence from, Britons' feelings and self-presentation.

Kumar and Bourdieu's writings on colonial and imperial identities are historical sociology, although their conceptions, and analytic uses, of time are somewhat different from those of the sociologists we examined in previous chapters. They are less concerned with tracing out the chains of contingent action that lead from the past to an outcome (such as capitalism or revolution) that they seek to explain. Rather, they begin with a major historical event, or more accurately a historical condition (imperialism), and trace out the implications of that social form for subsequent changes or lack of changes. In other words, rather than trying to explain the dynamic development or decline of the British or French empire, they begin with the fact of empire and look at how it affects social life along the dimensions that interest them the most, which are, for Kumar, political culture in the imperial metropole and, for Bourdieu, both economic development and ethnic relations in the French colony of Algeria.

Similarly, Philip Smith (2005) takes a culturalist approach to explaining why major powers in the era that followed the end of large formal empires after World War II embarked upon wars to assert or reinforce control over former colonies or areas of indirect rule. Like Kumar, Smith sees militarism as grounded in nationalist self-images and nationally specific narratives (which he labels "civil discourses") of dangers that justify war. He compares the US and Britain along with France and Spain, and his cases allow him to trace change over time. However, the changes he highlights are in the salience of cultural categories particular to each country. Smith has little to say about how change in America's or Britain's war-making capacities, the type of challenges from small countries and former colonies, or the overall structure of global geopolitics affects success in war or countries' willingness or capacity to begin or sustain wars.

Empires, like any other large-scale and complex social systems, cannot be comprehended if analyzed just as a cultural (or economic or military) formation. Often change begins in one realm and then affects another, which in turn impacts a third. Thus, a single-minded focus on culture (or any other realm) can lose key steps in the dynamics of change. Michael Mann (1986, 1993, 2012) offers a far more useful approach in his multi-volume history of power, in which he distinguishes among what he sees as the four principal forms of power: political, economic, military, and ideological. He argues that social actors and institutions gain leverage to the extent that they are able to marshal more than one sort of power. For example, the ancient Roman empire was more powerful and enduring than other ancient empires because it combined ideological power (a common Latin language and culture among elites) and economic power (trade networks that were more dense and enduring than those of any other ancient empire) along with the military power that undergirds all empires (Mann 1986, pp. 250–300).

Mann's key insight is that social change occurs in the "interstices" of the institutions in which power is held and exercised. Changes in the distribution of one type of power affect the other three types as well. In other words, when one power holder manages to co-opt or seize the power resources of others (which is what happens when an empire conquers a colony), the character of both the metropole and the colonies changes. Power holders can find that their ability to dominate subordinates or to apply their power within a territory is newly constrained or enhanced by transfers of power among others in which they did not directly participate. Thus, when a society becomes an empire, the expansion of (or creation of new) institutions of power abroad alters the existing structure of relations among elites and with the mass of people in the metropole.

Of course imperialism has an even greater effect on the social structure of conquered lands than it does on the metropole. Imperialists do not rule just with brute military force, although that often is vital to asserting and maintaining their authority. Rather, imperialists rule in large part indirectly, by inserting themselves and their institutions into existing political, economic, military, and ideological forms of power in their colonies. In that way, foreign imperialists alter the old institutions of power in conquered territories. Even when the empire withdraws from a colony (or in the many cases where foreigners do not establish formal control and instead rule indirectly), the institutions that remain in a post-colonial society do not revert to their pre-conquest state. That is why former empires often find it so easy to maintain dominance over their former colonies, even if they have withdrawn their military forces (and, of course, empires or hegemons often maintain bases in territories they do not formally rule). The institutions of the new post-independence state are still marked by the era of colonial rule in ways that allow capitalists and cultural ideas to continue to hold sway, often through co-opted local elites.

Mann (2012) offers a model of how to trace the influence of a particular social form (such as imperialism, capitalism, the state) over long spans of time, and he applies that model to states (which we examine in the next chapter) as well as to empires. He addresses the fundamental questions of (1) why a few leading capitalist nations, which held commanding economic power, created or extended vast empires in the nineteenth century, and (2) why those empires were comprised in part of formal colonies and in part of nominally independent states that the great powers controlled indirectly. He explains the expanding borders of those empires, and the shifting balances within each between formal and informal control, by tracing over time the extent and institutional bases of each empire's military, political, economic, and ideological power.

Mann focuses his analysis on three empires – the British, American, and Japanese – from 1890 to 1945. He finds those empires were rarely profitable. "It was not simply an instrumentally rational drive for economic profit that drove imperialism forward. The emotional desire for glory, security-laden fear of rivals, local weakness, and opportunity egged on by particular interest groups . . . tempted them onward, one step at a time" (2012, p. 112). The interest groups varied among the imperial powers, each with a distinct "blend of corporations and states" (p. 127) and of popular willingness to support foreign wars and occupations (high in Japan, low in the US) and in the number of citizens willing to settle in colonies (again high in Japan and low in the US). Britain was unusual in that its colonization in this period was propelled mainly "by independent adventurers, trading companies, and settlers," while other areas were indirectly controlled by "British economic and financial expansion" (p. 128). The particular institutional constellations of power within each imperial country shaped its form of imperialism, and those various imperialisms combined to create a geopolitics in which a few countries directly or indirectly controlled almost the entire globe.

Mann (2003) also has examined the limitations and failures of the US "War on Terror." Unlike Smith, who focuses on the inconsistencies among the "binary codes" used to justify the war in Iraq, Mann places culture in context when he shows how America's overwhelming strength in military power is not matched by its capacities in the other forms of power. He then analyzes how US weakness in the political, economic, and ideological realms allows its allies as well as Iraqis to challenge American plans and ensures that regimes that have been conquered by US military force remain able to challenge American economic and political interests. Mann gains analytic leverage by being attentive not just to change over time, as Smith is, but by tracing the ways in which changes in one sort of power in one geographic location affect other forms of power and the overall structure of imperial dominance within single countries and in relations among nations.

Mann's focus is mainly on the empires themselves rather than on the conquered and dominated territories, and, since he is writing a world history, there is limited opportunity for him to engage in detailed comparisons. In this way his is similar to Wallerstein and Arrighi's analyses of the interplay between cycles in and the historical development of the world system to explain the demise of one hegemon and its replacement with another dominant capitalist power. We discussed in chapter 2 how their analysis is pitched at the level of the entire world system and is not well suited to explaining why individual countries or regions move among the core, semi-periphery, and periphery. Nor can their theory explain why a particular country or empire becomes hegemonic in one era and loses its position to what had been a lesser power.

The most systematic effort to show how empires affect colonial and post-independence economic development is James Mahoney's (2010) comparison of Spain's Latin American colonies, which are then contrasted with Britain and Portugal's American colonies. Mahoney's great innovation is to show systematically how the complexity of pre-colonial institutions affected the nature of colonialism and hence the degree of development under colonialism and then after independence. He traces the development of each territory colonized by the Spanish through four stages: the social institutions right before the Spanish conquerors arrived; the structure created in the first, mercantilist phase of Spanish rule; the somewhat altered state of colonial government under liberal Bourbon rule in the eighteenth century; and, finally, the post-independence social order.

Mahoney's careful reading of each country's history led him to the realization that, for some countries, most notably Chile and the countries of Central America, there was yet another moment of structural transformation caused by nineteenth-century wars. Mahoney explains how war allowed Chile and Costa Rica to make developmental strides that would not have happened in its absence, while for the rest of Central America war brought reactionary elites to power that retarded economic and social development up to the present and into the foreseeable future. In the case of Costa Rica, its insulation from wars in the rest of Central America allowed for the consolidation of liberal government.

For Chile, war was both an immediate economic stimulus and the way in which it added lands rich in nitrates to its territory. Mahoney's analysis complements Zeitlin's, which we saw in chapter 2. Mahoney identifies both the period when Chile's social structure was opened up by war and the long-term consequences for economic development. Zeitlin traces the internal political dynamic that was the actual causal motor of change: the new nitrate lands created a new mining elite, which disrupted the old elite and class relations and made possible the two civil wars that created a type of state and a slightly new set of Chilean elites, thus allowing some, though still limited, economic development.

For the other Spanish American countries, their relative positions were locked in after independence. Argentina's famous decline, from one of the richest countries in the world in the 1920s to its current position at well below the levels of even the poorest Western European countries, is in line with the overall decline of Spanish America in those decades. Argentina and Uruguay remain at the top of the Latin American hierarchy, just where they were one hundred years ago. Their long-ago trajectories as Habsburg Spanish mercantile peripheries that became core liberal colonies of Bourbon Spain still shape their continental and world positions and their levels of social development.

Mercantile colonialism established a particular type of polity, a system of exploitation that used coercive methods of labor control to extract raw materials (most importantly precious metals, but also agricultural products). The specifics of labor control varied depending on the social structure encountered by the initial conquistadors. While the system of rule varied, the ruling colonial elite shared a crucial characteristic across all the colonies: a tight linkage, which in practice amounted to a fusion, of officials, clerics, landlords, and merchants. What varied across colonies was the size of the elite and how firmly they were able to embed themselves in the conquered societies. The bigger, richer, more settled, and more complex the pre-colonial society, the more deeply the mercantilist colonial elite was able to plant itself, fend off challenges from both the Spanish crown and indigenous peoples, and profiteer at the expense of future development. Where the elite was spread thin, as in peripheral Argentina, the Bourbon crown found empty spaces – both geographic and structural – in which it could insert new liberal elites that fostered economic development. Mahoney has little to say about how colonies affected the metropole. The great strength of his analysis is that he has found a systematic way to differentiate pre-colonial societies and use the differences among them along several dimensions to explain varying Spanish and, in a comparative chapter, British and Portuguese strategies for controlling the peoples and lands of the colonies the Europeans conquered. In essence, he argues that differences among types of colonialism or among forms of imperial rule are made when colonizers arrive at and conquer indigenous peoples. They are not shaped beforehand by metropolitan politics and culture.

The breadth and richness of Mahoney's comparative historical analysis allows him to explain in a more rigorous way than ever before why it is so difficult for lands with dense, advanced polities that were colonized by Europeans ever to escape from a peripheral position. Mercantilist core colonies never could achieve higher economic development because, during their time under mercantilist rule, elites were established that could not be eliminated by liberal reforms. Liberalism mattered ultimately mainly for the former peripheries, by creating an opening for a new commercial elite in Argentina. For much of the colonial world liberalism arrived too late.

Empires, as Mann teaches us, are never exclusively economic or military or cultural creations. Yet studies that focus on one or two aspects of imperialism can offer great insight if, like Mahoney's, they create a conceptual structure that allows them to specify the causal role of the analyzed factors and therefore create a basis for showing when and how other social forces enter into the causal chain, as we just sketched for Zeitlin's analysis of Chilean politics.

George Steinmetz's (2007, 2008) research on German colonialism parallels Mahoney's in crucial ways. Like Mahoney, he compares colonies within a single empire, the German. Like Mahoney, he gives analytic priority to one aspect of imperialism: in Steinmetz's work, ideological power. The German empire is especially suited for examining culture. It was created later than those of the other European imperial powers (though not later than the US empire). Germany's colonies stand out because they contributed almost nothing to the country's economy: its empire was created mainly for prestige and at the behest of German elites, who fought with one another for power, prestige, and offices within the colonial administration rather than for financial loot. As a result, German colonial elites enjoyed more autonomy from metropolitan interests (because the colonies were worth so little) than their Spanish, French, or British counterparts. Thus, Steinmetz is able to show how colonial elites engage in ideological and bureaucratic competition for power without the confounding pressures of metropolitan financial interests.

What does Steinmetz find? First, colonial officials didn't arrive in conquered lands as individuals. Rather, they came as representatives of elites transplanted from home and maintained their distinct identities in the colonies. The three principal German elites, "the nobility, the propertied bourgeoisie, and the Bildungsbürgertum (i.e., the educated middle class)" (2008, p. 597), arrived in the colonies with distinct forms of capital that they deployed to gain control over the German colonial government. The main terrain of struggle was "native policy." Each elite made claims to "ethnographic expertise" based on the sort of cultural capital they brought to the colonies from Germany.

Steinmetz shows how "Drawn-out contests between different fractions of a splintered dominant class may prevent a field from being settled while enhancing its autonomy, as field-specific modes of action become more systematic and clearly defined" (2008, p. 600), and provide a basis for colonial elites, both individually and collectively, to "enhance their autonomy from the metropolitan state over time" (ibid., pp. 591–2). In other words, while the three German elites fought with one another over how to deal with natives, they fought on the basis of expert knowledge, which they claimed was refined through first-hand experience in ruling over the particular natives of the colonies they inhabited. As each elite asserted expert knowledge, they were able collectively to distinguish themselves ever more decisively from their putative superiors, from the metropolitan elites that lobbied officials back in Berlin, and from elites in other colonies who, because they ruled different sorts of natives, had different expertise that could not be automatically transferred to another colony. The colonial elites used their claims of expertise to prevent metropolitan Germans from interfering in colonial policies directly or from exerting indirect influence by allying with one colonial elite against the others in return for policy decisions or for a share of the colonial spoils. This was evidenced in the growing capacity of colonial officials to take actions that were inimical to the interests of metropolitan capitalists, or even to the central German government's geopolitical interests. It also is demonstrated by the very different native policies officials pursued in Southwest Africa (where the Germans committed genocide), Samoa (where the natives were treated as anthropological curiosities), and Qingdao (where Chinese culture was respected even as the population was exploited economically and subordinated politically) – differences that can't be derived from economic or geopolitical considerations.

Steinmetz shows how colonial rule and native policies change over time and vary across colonies. Because he is so careful to specify the particular conditions of the German empire overall and the differences among each colony, his work, like Mahoney's, provides a basis for other scholars to examine how the ways in which elites deploy cultural capital in other empires affect systems of rule. Steinmetz's focus on comparing colonies does not provide a basis to examine how colonies and the German elites created by colonialism affect politics or economics in the metropole. That is due in large part to the particularities of the German empire – that it mattered so little to the German economy. The advantages of that case for revealing crucial dynamics in the colonies is a drawback to explicating the dynamics of an empire's effect on domestic political economy.

Although neither Steinmetz nor Mahoney makes this argument themselves, their work offers a blueprint for addressing the problems Chakrabarty (2007) raised with what he described as universalistic and Eurocentric scholarship. Neither Steinmetz nor Mahoney offers a universalistic theory of imperialism. Of course, their work is about Europeans since, in the centuries they are examining, Europeans were the imperialists. However, they are constantly alert to, and always carefully specify, the particular conditions that produced the variable forms of colonialism they describe and explain. Although neither of them focuses on resistance to colonial rule, their research provides a basis for others to specify the conditions that foster or inhibit independence movements.

We need to be careful not to allow the valid criticisms Chakrabarty and others offer of Eurocentrism to dissuade us from engaging in comparative analysis. Efforts at universalism, like Eisenstadt's (which manages to be universalistic without being Eurocentric, since it is based largely on ancient empires and China, not the modern European empires), that are inattentive to differences among empires do not further our understanding of the particular historical dynamics of each empire. On the other hand, Mann's theory, which is universalistic only in the sense that he agues that all societies are shaped by the interplay of the same four types of power, counteracts other types of universalism by showing how the mix of, and structural relations among, holders of each type of power vary across time and place. That provides the basis for specifying the range of commonalities, and for constructing explanations that fit the unique conditions of each empire, state, class, colony, or resistance movement. Chakrabarty's work is long on admonitions; unfortunately his actual empirical work is impressionistic and doesn't really provide a basis either for explanations of historical change or for variation across societies.

More useful are the writings of Julian Go and Karen Barkey, with whom I will conclude this chapter. They each address the problem of how to draw comparisons across historical eras and between empires. Go compares the British and US empires. He makes the crucial point that we must "compare [empires] across comparable historical phases" (2011, p. 21). Thus, we should compare the US and British empires not at the same moment, but rather at the times when each was in "hegemonic assent," "hegemonic maturity," or "decline." Go shows that empires in assent pursue different strategies to control colonies than do mature hegemons, and that empires face very different pressures when in decline. At the same time, his careful attention to phases of empire allows him to specify the differences between the British and US empires and to locate the sources of those differences: the sorts of territories they conquered (which is similar to Mahoney's analysis), their domestic economies, class structures, and state institutions, and also the different world historic eras in which each underwent imperial rise, dominance, and fall.

Go's analysis is different from that of world systems theorists because he shows how an empire's institutional and cultural forms, which were established before that empire achieved hegemony, determine how it is able to take advantage of the opportunities that world hegemony gives to deepen its imperial exploitation, and how empires employ those long-standing structures to manage their loss of hegemony. For Go, imperial policy is shaped by, but not derived from, a polity's geographic and temporal location in the world system. He brings imperialists back into the study of empire and shows how those actors inhabit institutions and possess beliefs and practices that variously limit or enhance their abilities to navigate geopolitical flux.

Karen Barkey (2008) links together a concern with the dynamics of empire (Go's focus) with the legacies of imperialism for former colonies (Mahoney's concern). She seeks to identify the causes of imperial disintegration and then traces how the legacies of empire shape the nation-states that are created in the wake of imperial collapse. Barkey's research is focused on the Ottoman empire. It is an appropriate case for her concerns, and her historical investigation of the Ottomans made clear the need to study the dynamics and consequences of collapse. Barkey, like Steinmetz, gains analytic leverage by picking a case in which external factors play a limited role. Just as Steinmetz examines colonies with little economic or geopolitical value to isolate the role of culture, Barkey's Ottoman empire was felled mainly by internal conflicts and contradictions rather than by external challenges.

How does Barkey examine the Ottoman empire's internal dynamics? She begins by taking seriously a truism in most scholars' accounts of empire: that empires are collections of largely autonomous ethnicities and local political units. She then asks: Why did the empire hold together at all, what strategies did the Ottoman rulers use to control territory and extract revenues, and how did those rulers decide (or how were they compelled) to abandon their desires for greater control?

Barkey finds that "the Ottomans understood well the limits of their rule, in terms of both the geographical reach of their control and their limited manpower, and fashioned an empire that was based on organizational diversity . . . accepting of multiple systems of rule, multiple negotiated frontiers, laws and courts, forms of revenue management, and religious diversity" (2008, p. 70). Ottoman rulers had the most control over the army. Soldiers, many of whom were recruited from out-groups (slaves, conquered and kidnapped Christian children, Greeks), were rewarded with grants of land that often were seized from hereditary aristocrats. However, armies cost money, and therefore the Ottomans had to adopt a strategy Barkey characterizes as "fiscalism," the effort to maximize revenues. In this the Ottoman sultans were similar to other pre-capitalist imperial rulers in that they needed a constant stream of money to pay off their supporters, as well as to keep armies in the field to suppress opposition, to repel rival powers, and to keep the whole enterprise going by expanding the empire's territory; yet, unlike capitalist imperialists, they generated very little revenue from trade or by directly exploiting the economies of conquered territories.

Barkey, by tracing this strategy over time, shows both why the Ottomans were able to sustain their rule for so long and why their strategy ultimately failed. Sultans were granted lifetime tax farms in return for one-time payments in moments of fiscal crisis. Tax farmers, secure in their positions, were able to ally with merchants and landlords (especially those to whom they granted or sold tax sub-farms), creating what Barkey calls "regional governance regimes" that were highly resistant to sultans' efforts to play elites off against one another, and thereby allowed tax farmers to keep more of their revenues. This worsened the fiscal crisis and also provided a basis for demands for autonomy and independence in peripheral areas, especially the Balkans. Autonomy became easier to pursue as merchants in the empire were able to link to capitalists in the evolving world system based in Europe. In this way, Barkey is able to specify the role of capitalism and of the world system in the empire's downfall.

Barkey's mode of analysis and her efforts to specify the ways in which ethnicity and nationalism affected the Ottoman empire provide a template for her and others (Barkey and von Hagen 2008) to analyze the demise of the Habsburg, Russian, and Soviet empires along with the Ottomans. This work provides a basis to trace the long-term influence of empires and colonialism on state formation. It is to states that we turn in the next chapter.

5
States

States have reorganized the global landscape of power over the past several centuries. Empires have broken apart into nation-states. Power, which once was decentralized and held by kin groups, tribes, city-states, corporate bodies, churches, and other overlapping, competing entities, has become concentrated into states that claim (and increasingly have been able to enforce) a monopoly on violence and also on legal authority within internationally recognized boundaries. At the same time as they have taken power from rival entities, states have demanded a growing array of resources from their subjects (taxes, military service, attendance in schools, obedience to a growing set of laws and regulations), while citizens have been able to claim a lengthening list of rights from their states (voting rights, legal equality, social welfare benefits, education, protection from natural and man-made disasters, and more).

The main difficulty encountered by historical sociologists is not in tracing or documenting changes in state capacities and obligations over time or in specifying differences among states. Rather, the complexity is in identifying causality. States were formed and transformed at the same time as capitalism became the dominant mode of production, and as family and community structures, demographic and residential patterns, technology, and ideology all underwent fundamental transformations. How can historical sociologists disentangle these overlapping and interrelating changes? How can they determine causality? When is it useful to study a single case in a theoretically informed way, and when are cross-country and/or temporal comparisons necessary?

Our goal in this chapter is not to review the vast literatures that seek to address the various facets of states formation and development. (You can find reviews of those debates in Lachmann 2010, along with my evaluations of which answers are most convincing and which lines of research most fruitful.) Rather, this chapter will focus on a few of the most compelling treatments of two problems – (1) state formation and (2) the emergence and consolidation of varying systems of social benefits – to identify the most productive ways to address questions of historical causality.

State Formation

State formation occurred, as we noted above, at the same time as capitalism developed. How are those two transformations causally related? We saw in chapter 2 that Perry Anderson (1974) used cross-country comparisons to argue that they were linked by the ruling class of each era. First, the feudal ruling class formed absolutist states to address their difficulties in controlling peasants after the Black Death. Then absolutist states in Western, but not Eastern, Europe fostered the formation of a new bourgeois class. The bourgeoisie then staged revolutions that overthrew absolutism in favor of new, bourgeois states that furthered capitalist development and the growth of the bourgeoisie.[12] Thus, for Anderson, class actors are the causal link between state formation and the transition to capitalism, with each causal step occurring when either a new class is formed or an existing class adopts a new mode of class struggle.

Anderson's analysis is elegant since he identifies a consistent mechanism (class conflict) and a consistent set of actors (classes) to explain all the outcomes, thereby linking together state formation and capitalist development. Unfortunately, his model suffers, as we saw in chapter 2, from his inability to explain how similar absolutist states and class conflict yielded a bourgeois revolution in England a century and a half before that of France. Nor can he account for the differences in the post-revolutionary states and in the dimensions and pace of capitalist development in the two countries – weaknesses revealed by his cross-country comparisons.

Charles Tilly also identifies a consistent set of actors as the agents of change in both the economic and the political realm. In contrast to Anderson, Tilly's key actors are not classes but instead elites that control the state. In Tilly's account, power in pre-state Europe (and indeed throughout the world) was diffused in the hands of nobles, clerics, and others who commanded small and overlapping political units. Beginning five hundred years ago in Europe, some of those power holders managed to mobilize the resources needed to attack, defeat, and incorporate rival elites, thereby amalgamating "something like 500 states, would-be states, stateless, and statelike organizations" into "a mere 25 to 28 states" by 1990 (Tilly 1990, pp. 42–3 and *passim*).

State elites needed armed men and bureaucrats to control their expanding territories. Tilly argues that places where capitalism (or at least markets) had already begun to develop were "capital rich," meaning they had residents with money who were easier to tax (because their money was more liquid than that of farmers). The lucky rulers who controlled such territories had more revenue than rulers of economically backward territories, and so could afford to hire more mercenary soldiers and then, more often than not, defeat the smaller armies of cash-poor rivals and absorb their territories. This argument allows Tilly to link together the causation of state formation and capitalism. Capitalism aids state formation. The weakness of Tilly's model is that he offers no explanation for why capitalism or market economies developed earlier in some parts of Europe than elsewhere. Nor does he have much to say about how states further capitalist development, except for noting that (1) states buy weapons that expand the manufacturing sector and that (2) when peasants are taxed they need to raise cash, which forces them to market their agricultural products and/or search for wage labor. This commercialized agriculture and also draws peasants off the land to become proletarians.

Tilly carefully notes that conscription reduced the advantage of capital-rich states. States with large numbers of subjects, and the bureaucratic capacity to draft them, could overwhelm rich rivals that once dominated Europe. Thus, in the eighteenth century, Italian city-states or the Netherlands lost their military edge to populous nations such as Russia or France. Indeed, once revolutionary France became the first country to conscript hundreds of thousands and then millions of citizens, small, cash-rich polities were reduced to bit players in European geopolitics. Among the surviving large states, the most successful combined market economics that made them capital rich with large populations that could be conscripted by regimes that also were coercion rich. France is the leading example of this happy (happy for the rulers, not the citizens) combination. Britain, which did not conscript soldiers until the middle of World War I, used its money to subsidize poorer coercion-rich allies to build the coalition that ultimately defeated Napoleon.

The second part of Tilly's story to some extent reverses the causality of the first half. If early market economies fostered state formation, then strong states stimulated later capitalist development. States and capitalism were interlinked, and the developmental level of each determines, in Tilly's model, the direction, strength, and specific impact of the causal effect. Remember, in chapter 1 we saw that Tilly contends that social processes are path dependent. Here we see how the path dependence of state formation affects capitalism and vice versa. As capitalism develops, it directs state formation down particular, capital-rich paths, and, as states become stronger, they push capitalist development in certain directions.

Tilly adds another element to the interrelation of states and capitalism. While for much of his career he identified capital and coercion as the dominant assets for, and constraints upon, state elites, in *Trust and Rule* (2005) he showed that "trust networks," which can be based on kin, religion, trade relations, or other ideological or structural bases, were another resource which state elites sought to control. For most of human history, trust networks stood apart from states and other large-scale political units. Yet, capitalism weakened trust networks. Proletarians were drawn to cities, away from the tight communities that protected trust networks. In addition, capitalist markets created volatility and risks that trust networks lacked the material or organizational resources to guard against. This created an opening for states to offer social benefits to proletarians in return for loyalty (above all, a willingness to serve in the armed forces). As states absorbed trust networks, the leverage over the state of aristocrats and other privileged elites declined, creating an opening for proletarians (often led by conscripts and their families) to demand democratic rights as well as social benefits. Thus, Tilly identifies yet another path, through trust networks, by which capitalism strengthens the state, and the enhanced power of the state further shapes capitalism (through an expanded proletariat, social benefits, and democracy).

For Tilly, the state is the organizational pivot, the site where all varieties of resources are drawn in and redeployed in ways that reshape the capitalist economy and a civil society once based on trust. Tilly's approach has the advantage of being comprehensive: he integrates the transformation of all the major social forces within a single, state-centered model. His approach is limited in a way similar to the shortcomings of Anderson's Marxist model: neither can account for variations within nation-states because they elide over conflict within what each presents as a coherent actor: Anderson's aristocratic and bourgeois classes and Tilly's state elite.

Not surprisingly, theoretical elegance and temporal coherence are won by simplifying history. The question is what is lost in the simplification in which each historical sociologist must engage in order to create a coherent narrative from rich historical evidence to clarify overlapping and interlocking causalities. If the cost of simplification is an inability to explain the object of one's analysis, such as Anderson's inability to account for England's early bourgeois revolution, then simplification has been taken too far. In Tilly's case, what is lost is somewhat peripheral to his inquiry: the differences in the sorts of citizenship rights states offer, or are forced to concede, to their subjects.

Tilly writes of the "bargains" struck between rulers and trust communities, but he does not explain how those bargains were reached or how the terms of those bargains varied across time and place. Nor does he relate the terms of those bargains to the later developments of welfare states. It is unfair to ask a scholar to address topics beyond the scope of his or her study: thus, we can't expect Tilly to explain the welfare state when his interest is state formation. However, we can evaluate a theory or approach on the basis of whether it can be adapted to explain matters beyond those for which it was developed. On those terms, Tilly's model of state formation can be critiqued for its inability to link either the process of state formation or the relationship between states in formation and the popular protests and resistance they provoke[13] to the development of citizenship rights or social benefits.

The origins of citizenship rights, and how these are related causally to the development of capitalism and the formation of states, is precisely the subject of Margaret Somers's (1993, 2008) research. As we examine her analysis, we will see that she provides a way to account for national differences, and for differences within countries, that are obscured in Tilly's work, and thereby offers a template for explaining variations among countries in social welfare systems, even though her study is of a single country.

Somers (1993) finds that citizenship rights varied across localities in Britain, and that classes or smaller groups (Tilly's trust communities) also differed locally in the demands they made for civil rights (due process, the right to sell one's labor), political rights (voting), and social rights (public education, welfare benefits). She notes that not all the bourgeoisie demanded property rights, nor did all workers seek social benefits; nor were civil and voting rights demanded or secured everywhere before social benefits were fought over.

Claims varied according to the characteristics of local communities more than they did by aggregate classes within nations. Variation was chiefly geographic because demands were made and fought for within communities. The capacities of communities to articulate and fight for rights were built upon, and therefore differed in terms of, their inheritance systems (some of which fostered intergenerational cohesion, while others pushed disinherited younger sons to migrate, disrupting community ties) and in the structure of their apprenticeship systems. Inheritance and apprenticeship systems, in turn, shaped local governmental structures, which determined the power of local elites and their relationship to the national government and also defined the opportunities for ordinary citizens to create a civil society.

Somers sees the British legal system as plastic – something created and continually altered out of a history of struggles over land rights and labor relations. Thus, even within a unified polity, such as that of Britain, there can be varying definitions of citizenship and different arrays of rights claimed by individuals and communities. What citizenship rights, and later social benefits, each community is able to claim and achieve is a function of that community's institutional assets and the social relations among inhabitants. Thus, Somers shows that the British "state" is in fact a shifting amalgamation of localized institutions, practices, and social relations.

As the complex relations among local communities, individuals, and the state change, citizenship rights can be lost as well as gained. Waves of democracy have, in certain eras, been followed by waves of dictatorship (Markoff 1996a), and today neoliberalism is weakening or eliminating social benefits in some countries. These benefits wax and wane in states that in Tilly's terms all enjoy high capacities for extracting revenues, waging wars, and controlling their citizens. Thus, the analysis of social benefits, to which we now turn, cannot be understood merely by applying modes of analysis used to explain state formation. Rather, we need to pay attention to the ways in which social groups can mobilize resources and make ideological claims to citizenship against both capitalist markets and the state. Somers argues that, where citizenship rights are strong, the state takes, or is compelled by active citizens to take, the side of citizens against market forces: "the fragile project of sustaining socially inclusive democratic rights requires the countervailing powers of a social state, a robust pubic sphere to hold it accountable, and a relationally sturdy public society" (Somers 2008, p. 5). Mobilized citizens can alter the relationship between state formation and capitalist development, and between state elites and capitalists, with profound consequences for social benefits.

Social Benefits

States confer social benefits. If we look around the world, most old-age pensions, health care, education, childcare, and other benefits are administered and paid for through states. Even in the United States, where employers provide the majority of citizens with health insurance, those benefits are subsidized indirectly through the tax code by the federal government, which also closely regulates those plans. The same is true for private pensions.

Yet it is a mistake to talk about the state as a coherent organization headed by a unified elite. States are created, and their capacities increase, because multiple elites (as well as non-elites) come together within state institutions for a variety of motives (Lachmann 2010, pp. 62–6 and *passim*). At the same time as states "increase their infrastructural power . . . the institutional capacity of a central state . . . to penetrate its territories and logistically implement decisions," so too do "civil society parties" gain in their capacity "to control the state" (Mann 1993, p. 59). We can't just track the state's ability to control civil society; we need to trace the ways in which political power and conflicts move from civil society into, and become about, the multiple institutions of the state.

How do Mann's rubric of state types and his four forms of power contribute to an understanding of the development of social benefits and their variability across states? Mann alerts us to the necessity of finding the institutional sites at which each group of actors mobilizes its power. Since states are repositories of all four types of power, each increase in a class or other social group's capacity to exercise one or more forms of power affects the overall structure of power and the ability of those groups to force the state to offer social benefits. It also affects the state's infrastructural capacity actually to fulfill social groups' demands for benefits.

Mann offers his analysis at a highly general level, and his chapter on the expansion of the nineteenth-century state's "civilian scope" mainly sketches differences between the US, Britain, France, and Germany (1993, pp. 479–509). Yet, his work suggests a clear plan for how to conduct comparative historical research on social benefits.

- *First*, identify groups that demanded social benefits. Here Mann differs from Somers, who saw such demands form at the local level in ways that responded to groups' local capacities to define themselves and mobilize. Mann instead looks to national politics, and sees the working class as the dominant actor for expansion of the state's social programs in the nineteenth century.
- *Second*, specify how the targets of those demands (capitalists or state elites) reacted to such demands. Mann's conception of the state as disorganized and divided makes us sensitive to the possibility that such demands do not provoke a unified response, that, when the working class applies pressure, state elites can divide or can come into conflict with capitalists.
- *Third*, examine how the establishment of social programs affects state capacities to mobilize the various types of power for objectives in other realms – e.g., whether the state's military capacity is enhanced or retarded by the establishment of old-age pensions.
- *Fourth*, examine how new social programs affect the subsequent capacities of social groups to mobilize or of state elites and capitalists to resist future demands.

These four analytic steps together produce a dynamic model of the interactions among politics within states, relations between actors in the state and those in civil society, and the growth, stagnation, or retraction of social benefits. This strategy is historical in that the interests and capacities of various power holders, and of those making demands upon them, have different effects as the actions, capacities, and structural relations of all the other actors change over time.

Mann's approach is very different from that of Piven and Cloward (1971), whom we encountered in chapter 3. They see the interests and demands of the poor as largely unchanging and the responses of the state to disorder as consistent over time. Their goal is to account for social welfare benefits, and they do not examine in any depth how the creation of such benefits changes the state or look at other factors that can interact with protests and changes in governmental social benefits to affect the wider landscape of power and social relations. As a result, Piven and Cloward are unable to account for differences in the programs established by the US state in the 1930s and the 1960s, and other scholars have not been able to correlate the level of protests by workers or the poor with social benefits in other countries (Skocpol and Amenta 1986).

Social benefits are not just elite responses to eruptions of popular demands. Rather, social programs are created through complex interactions that reflect the historically created interests and capacities of various power holders. We need to see how those capacities and interests come together in each particular time and place.

Yet, we do not have to despair and assume that the particularities of each case prevent us from finding patterns of historical change. Gøsta Esping-Andersen (1990) offers a model of how historical sociology can construct causal explanations of differences in national social welfare policies. Esping-Andersen looks at the array of power holders and mass groups involved in politics in eighteen wealthy industrialized societies in Europe, North America, and Asia. He is concerned with explaining how countries became locked into one of three "social welfare-state regimes" in the twentieth century. Note that his question is carefully focused. Esping-Andersen has identified a limited time span for each country when social welfare programs were enacted and finds that, once instituted, they change very little in form even if the scope of benefits expands (or, in recent years, contracts).

This finding leads Esping-Andersen to focus his analysis on the political constellation in each country when social welfare policies were instituted. He identifies distinct political alliances in each type of social welfare regime. In "conservative" countries, powerful and relatively autonomous state elites, often created centuries earlier under absolutism, ally with religious bodies to create state-financed programs that often are administered through churches and other existing corporatist bodies. Churches are key, since they disrupt the farmer–worker alliances that overwhelmed capitalist opposition in countries that created social democratic regimes. Liberal countries (such as the US, Britain, and Japan) had neither a strong state nor an enduring farmer–worker alliance and so got fragmented and means-tested government programs combined with private pension and health plans.

Esping-Andersen looks at types of power holders but does not distinguish among types of power in the formal way Mann does. He does examine the institutions controlled by each type of power holder and by groups in civil society (especially farmers, workers, church members). What is most valuable in his work is that he is able both to identify the historical moments when groups were able to take effective action and create social welfare policies and to link causally the form and content of those policies to (1) the characteristics of the actors who demanded or granted social benefits, (2) the structures of alliances among political antagonists, and (3) the institutions through which antagonists mobilized and through which benefits were ultimately administered. His method also allows us to see why, after the periods of welfare state formation, policies have proven to be so enduring. Esping-Andersen's approach is analogous to Paige's (1997) explanation of why Costa Rica was unique in Central America in creating an advanced social welfare system (discussed in chapter 3). Paige identifies the actors who transformed the Costa Rican state and then shows how the new state structure stabilized politics in ways that limited each class and the state elite from pursuing further transformation. Similarly, Haggard and Kaufman (2008) identify elite and class coalitions that created social welfare regimes in Latin America, Eastern Europe, and East Asia that are similar to those in Esping-Andersen's three types.

Esping-Andersen gains analytic power by looking at the welfare state as a whole and arguing that the entire complex of a nation's politics produces a welfare regime that shapes programs in all substantive areas, including old-age pensions, disability, health care and childcare. Skocpol and her collaborators, as well as critics who have engaged her in debate, adopt a different strategy: examining a single social welfare provision (old-age pensions or nationally guaranteed health care) and trying to account for differences in the timing of when those policies were instituted in various nations.

The debate over old-age pensions shows what can be accomplished through a focus on timing. (The key contributors to this debate, in order of their publications, are Orloff and Skocpol 1984; Quadagno 1984; Skocpol and Amenta 1985; Quadagno 1985; Domhoff 1986; Quadagno 1986;

Jenkins and Brents 1989.) Orloff and Skocpol ask why old-age pensions were instituted three decades earlier in Britain than in the US. Their answer focuses on the two states' capacities to administer (or to be perceived by the public as being able to administer) a national pension program without political bias or corruption. They conclude that earlier timing reflects greater state capacity. Quadagno argues instead that the Great Depression created class mobilization, and also divisions among capitalists, that made it possible to pass the Social Security Act. Quadagno has little to say about Britain; her focus on the US leaves open the question of what macro-events, if any, altered British politics to allow for the passage of their old-age pensions. The subsequent back and forth between Skocpol and Quadagno and the other contributors focuses on the extent to which a significant group of US capitalists supported the New Deal in general and social security in particular, or if state elites were able to create that program on their own or by enlisting non-capitalists who mobilized in protest movements or through the Democratic Party.

This debate over social security advanced as the contributors were able to show how actors within the state strengthened their positions by building ideological, political, and economic ties to groups in civil society. They are limited by their general inability to show how the state elite and state policies affected social relations in civil society. Somers's great contribution was to clarify the interaction, the two-way causal flow between state and civil society. Similarly, Mann's conceptual framework is designed precisely to show how state and civil society affect and reorder each other over time.

The limitations of Skocpol and Quadagno's approaches to social security are due in large part to their efforts to explain a single policy episode rather than present a long-term narrative of political change in the US. The shortcomings of their work on social security are surmounted when they address government health policy. Because their goal is to explain the absence of policy innovation (the US's unique failure to create a national health-care system even though every other wealthy country had done so decades earlier) rather than the passage of a piece of legislation, Skocpol and Quadagno are forced to look at long-term political processes. Although they differ in their analyses, Skocpol (1996) and Quadagno (2004) agree that the lack of a national health-care system in the US, along with the federal programs that were enacted (above all, Medicare and Medicaid, which were instituted in 1965 and have been expanded and revised since then), has reconfigured both the economics of the health-care industry and the political interests and alliances of groups that mobilize to create or block national health care. The decisive power of private insurance firms to block Clinton's health-care plan, and then to shape and help to passage Obama's legislation (Jacobs and Skocpol 2010), was the product of a chain of contingent events that transformed the relationship among physicians, hospitals, and insurance companies, and thereby shaped each of those groups' interests and their capacities to act politically alone or in alliance with others.

Monica Prasad (2006) takes a similar macroscopic approach to explain the different neoliberal policies adopted in the US, Britain, France, and Germany. Her goal is to explain why each country adopted certain policies but not others. Unlike Skocpol and Quadagno, Prasad is not trying to explain American uniqueness. Nor does she simplistically see neoliberalism as a tidal wave that swamps progressive forces in all countries. Instead, she engages in rigorous comparative historical analysis by focusing on "policy episodes" – moments when specific legislation or regulatory policies are enacted in a country. Prasad asks what happened before each episode to make the neoliberal initiative possible in that country, and what it was about the political balance of forces and governmental structure that blocked similar steps in other countries. For example, why were tax cuts enacted in the US and Britain but not in France or Germany, while state-owned firms were privatized in France and Britain, but not in Germany or the US?

Prasad looks at how links were constructed in each country between public officials and state-owned enterprises, on the one hand, and private entities and interests groups in civil society, on the other. That provides a basis for her to identify moments when those alliances were disrupted, creating openings for government officials, parties, and private interest groups, or, in the US, policy entrepreneurs with only weak links to parties, to push ahead with neoliberal initiatives.

Change, or the ability to resist change, thus cannot be understood in terms of either state capacities or the power and mobilization of interest groups alone. Instead, Prasad looks at the entire complex of political forces and relations to find the sites of change at particular moments. In that way she is able to explain why only a few episodes of neoliberal policy change occurred in each country, and why the policies differed so much from country to country despite the rising ideological sway of neoliberal ideas in all four countries.

States are not unitary organizations; nor is there a single state elite. The best historical sociology of the state allows us to see how the boundaries between state and civil society shift over time and how groups both find unity and identity and conceive and reconceive their interests and allies. All of this is contingent, and contingency can be seen in cross-country comparisons as well as in single-country studies (such as that by Somers). The goal for historical sociologists is not just to trace chains that culminate in new social policies (or the repeal or retrenchment of such policies), citizenship rights, or wars and declarations of independence, but to see the entire social landscape in which actors are simultaneously within and outside of the state and in which the borders between the two are complex and shifting.

6
Inequality

The dominant sociological approach to inequality focuses on individuals and tries to identify the personal characteristics (family background, race, scores on IQ tests, educational attainment) that can account for differences in income or "socioeconomic status." Some historical sociologists and historians adopt the same methodology, conducting studies of "status attainment" in past societies (Thernstrom 1964; Wrightson and Levine 1979; and Levine and Wrightson 1991 are among the most sophisticated examples). Yet, whether contemporary or historical, this approach does not ask how the array of hierarchical positions into which individuals are slotted came into existence. Nor – and this is the crucial failing – does a focus on individuals provide a basis to explain, or even to trace, changes in the overall structure of stratification. Some people are going to end up better off than most, and others worse off. If we want to understand why a particular person ends up on a particular rung of the ladder, then the methods and data of status attainment are useful. However, if we want to understand why the rungs of the ladder are more widely spaced at some moments of history, or why the fraction of a society's population on any particular rung increases or decreases, or to identify the moments and causes of change, the focus on individual characteristics is largely worthless. Instead we need to engage in cross-national and temporal comparisons or theoretically informed case studies to reveal the dynamics of historical change.

Charles Tilly, in *Durable Inequality* (1998), offers another critique of status attainment. He notes that "large, significant inequalities in advantages among human beings correspond mainly to categorical differences such as black/white, male/female, citizen/foreigner, or Muslim/Jew rather than to individual differences in attributes, propensities, or performances" (p. 7). Tilly praises "individualistic analyses" for specifying "the outcomes" – i.e., the degree of inequality – but "they have, however, relied on obscure, implausible, or insufficient causal mechanisms grounded in individual experience and action" (p. 21). Instead, he advocates looking for similarities in the processes by which inequalities grounded in various distinctions (race, gender, class, ethnicity, kin) are created and sustained. Tilly identifies four such mechanisms: "exploitation by the elite, opportunity hoarding by the nonelite, emulation, and adaptation" (p. 26). He contends: "People who create or sustain categorical inequality by means of the four basic mechanisms rarely set out to manufacture inequality as such. Instead they solve other organizational problems by establishing categorical unequal access to valued outcomes" (p. 11).

Tilly's model is historical in that he shows how the four mechanisms reinforce, modify, or occasionally undermine one another. Thus, the degree and durability of inequality is determined not by the extent of one group's prejudice but by the extent to which the four mechanisms interact to compound their effects. Tilly uses South Africa as one of his main examples. He traces how apartheid developed out of the ways in which existing exploitation, centered on the mining industry, melded with opportunity hoarding by non-elite whites and then was emulated in other economic and governmental sectors. Tilly is making an anti-culturalist argument: contingent events created extreme inequality which then led white South Africans to adopt racist beliefs and behaviors. A culture of racism did not cause apartheid; instead a structure of inequality fortified and sustained racism, which provided the political support to institutionalize formal apartheid.

Tilly's analytic methodology can be contrasted with that of Anthony Marx (1998), a political scientist who compares the divergent racial categories created in the nineteenth and twentieth century in the US, South Africa, and Brazil. Marx sees the emerging nation-states in all three as the key causal force in creating each country's system of racial inequality: US and South African state elites used racism to create solidarity among non-elite whites who were in conflict with one another, while the Brazilian state did not create racial categories because it did not need to foster white solidarity, since there already was harmony, or at least a lack of overt conflict, among whites. Since Marx identifies just a single mechanism to explain racial inequality, he is unable to account for later changes in white–black inequality. Instead, he argues that, once the pattern of racial relations was set, it determined the extent of black mobilization in the three countries in subsequent decades.[14]

What is lost in Marx's analysis is what is made possible in Tilly's: the ability to trace a two-way dynamic between conflicts among elites and non-elites within the dominant, white, race, and then to use that dynamic to account for changes in inter-racial inequality over time. Tilly's model also is better able to account for when and where the exploited (such as blacks in the US and South Africa) mobilize against those who exploit them, or who hoard opportunities at their expense, and provides a basis to specify how resistance by the oppressed affects the mechanisms for generating inequality. In the real world, the exploiters whom the oppressed challenge are not a cohesive group. Resistance by the exploited and excluded affects relations among those above them, creating dynamics that produce effects that often were not desired or anticipated by any of the antagonists.

Tilly's framework for analyzing resistance to inequality also is more sophisticated than Marx's. Resistance, in Tilly's analysis, is fostered by the very categories (race, religion, gender, etc.) that the dominant group uses to identify those whom they exploit and exclude. Blacks in South Africa, for example, came to think of themselves and organize in terms of race as the state and whites in civil society increasingly exploited them in those terms. Tilly's model derives change in the degree and form of resistance from the organization of exploitation and exclusion, not from the severity of inequality, as Marx does. In this, Tilly's approach is compatible with Somers's analysis of mobilization for citizenship, while Marx's is closer to Piven and Cloward's image of social movements, which we examined in the previous chapter. Tilly's model also provides a basis for analyzing how concessions to exploited groups (such as Britain's grant of citizenship rights to Catholics) affects future resistance – why in some cases it can heighten political action by exploited groups (such as US blacks in the Civil Rights era) or push it in new directions (toward Irish nationalism after the achievement of British citizenship), while in other cases concessions actually succeed in quieting opposition. None of those outcomes can be predicted or explained by measuring inequality along the dimensions of income, wealth, legal rights, or social status.

Tilly himself never wrote a sustained case study or comparative work that used the categories and mode of analysis he developed in *Durable Inequality*. Nor, despite the fact that *Durable Inequality* won the American Sociological Association's Distinguished Scholarly Publication Award (i.e., best book award) in 2000, has the book inspired scholars to research a topic or attempt to solve a problem using its framework. Go to Google Scholar and take a look at the authors who cite this book. Most of them mention Tilly in passing, or how his concepts are like the ones they developed on their own or drew from other theoretical works. In contrast, Tilly's work on social movements and state formation has sparked extensive and rich scholarship by numerous students and admirers. This gap in research is disappointing, but it also opens a fruitful agenda for future scholars.

Unfortunately, the individualistic focus continues to dominate research on inequality. Let us see how this focus has distorted and limited sociologists' efforts to explain the drastic increase in inequality of income and wealth in the US in recent decades. We then will look at some historical sociologists who have been successful at tracing and explaining shifts in inequality over time in various eras and parts of the world.

Inequality in the United States

Obviously, individuals care a great deal about their chances for mobility and whether they will rise or fall relative to their parents or to where they are today. Most of us want to know to what extent we can raise our lifetime incomes or social prestige through our own efforts, most notably by getting more education, and to what extent the writer Jimmy Breslin (1990, p. 103) was correct when he wrote that "most American success originates in an obstetrician's hands: if he pulls you out of a woman who is in the right marriage, your future is assured."

Our individual chances don't necessarily tell us much about the nature of our society, and they tell us very little about whether our society as a whole is changing in any significant way. At one extreme, we could live in a society with "numerous individual-level changes [that] nevertheless leave both the macropattern of relationships and the aggregate units intact (i.e. change within unchanging structures)" (Breiger 1990, p. 9). For the individuals in such a society, it matters greatly whether they are the ones going up or down, but the overall level of inequality, and even the distance between strata, can remain unchanged over long periods of time. As we will see below, peasant communities often exhibited this pattern.

At the other extreme, there can be little or no change in the relative standing of individuals in a society, while the gap between strata narrows or widens significantly. That pattern is true of the United States at the beginning of the twenty-first century. Intergenerational mobility in the US has declined sharply since 1980 (Aaronson and Mazumder 2007), even as inequality has risen drastically since the 1970s (Piketty and Saez 2007–12). In other words, Americans today are more likely than Americans forty years ago and more likely than Europeans today to remain in the same stratum from decade to decade and from one generation to the next. However, the economic consequences of being in each stratum have changed drastically over those years. Americans in the top 1 percent have increased their share of national income from under 9 percent in 1976 to 23.5 percent in 2007, equaling the previous peak set in 1928, and that gain has come entirely at the expense of the bottom 90 percent (ibid., table A3). Studies of individual life chances and mobility don't reveal those changes; only examining income and wealth distribution over decades can do that. It is revealing that Piketty and Saez, the two economists who have conducted this research, are French (although Saez currently teaches in the US). Few US economists or sociologists, including the scholars who have produced decades of status attainment research, have considered this topic worthy of their attention, and none have studied it with the rigor of Piketty and Saez.[15]

Historical sociological analysis is necessary if we want to explain the changes in wealth distribution documented by Piketty and Saez. The questions that need to be answered are: How do the rich keep getting richer? What has changed from the 1945–73 period, when incomes for the bottom 99 percent rose faster than for the top 1 percent? What have the top 1 percent managed to do since then to enrich themselves at the expense of everyone else, whose incomes and assets have hardly increased in the past forty years? To answer those questions requires placing data on inequality in the context of political and economic changes, making the study of inequality part of a broader sociology of change. Here is an agenda of research waiting for theoretically and historically minded sociologists. It is an agenda that can provide the basis for comparative study, to examine why a few other countries have paralleled the US in the concentration of wealth, while many others have had lesser concentration, and some have avoided this shift entirely.

How to Study Inequality Historically

Historical sociology can show how the overall structure of inequality has changed, worldwide and in individual countries, over the very long term. It also can identify moments of dramatic change in inequality and thereby focus attention on the causal sequences that culminate in great increases or decreases in inequality. Thus, historical sociologists of inequality can follow the same strategy we saw applied in previous chapters to explain causes of revolutions and social movements, state formation, the origins of capitalism, and other fundamental social changes: first identify the moment of significant change, and then look for causes in the period before that change.

We also need to be aware that money and prestige are not the only dimensions of inequality. Goran Therborn (2006) points out that life expectancy, human rights to freedom, and respect are as fundamental to the richness and meaning of human life as material possessions. He argues that each of the three has its own dynamics. Obviously, there is some link between income and life expectancy, for example; however, Therborn notes that we need to be alert to times and places where one of those dimensions diverges from the others or responds to distinct causal forces. Such divergences are most likely, in Therborn's view, among rather than within nations. The vast gaps in life expectancy that opened with the introduction of public health and access to plentiful food in rich (but not poor) countries in the nineteenth century have been greatly narrowed as public health has come to more of the world, even as the death rates between professional and manual workers have widened in recent decades in Britain and some other wealthy countries (Therborn 2006, pp. 20–2, 35–6; see also Sen 1992). Therborn's analysis is presented at a macroscopic level, and he doesn't examine the production of inequality at any location in detail. The causal forces he identifies operate on a national or global scale. His essay is more useful for sensitizing us to problems that can be addressed through historical analysis rather than in actually offering solutions himself.

Historical sociologists must overcome fundamental problems of conception and data if they want to engage in studies of inequality, and they must find ways to adapt causal models to the very different systems of stratification that existed in past societies and that still exist in some places in the world today. Data on income and wealth were rare and incomplete until the twentieth century. As we will see, historical studies of stratification often have to extrapolate from local and fragmentary data.[16] In any case, it is difficult to compare contemporary and historical data, since there are two fundamental differences between how income and wealth were accumulated in most historical societies and how they are understood in modern societies. First, until the advent of capitalism, property was not privately owned in the sense we understand it today. A feudal estate was not owned by anyone, and to regard it as the private property of a lord, or to regard a peasant farm as the property of the family that farmed it, is at odds with the reality that various families or corporate entities had overlapping income and use rights to land. Elsewhere, land was controlled by tribes whose chiefs did not own it any more than a US president owns the Pentagon or the Pope St Peter's. Second, until a few hundred years ago, families, not individuals, accrued income and held property (Adams 2005; we will examine her argument in more detail in the next chapter on gender). Familial claims limited the ability of an individual to spend or alienate the family property and molded each family member's efforts to earn income or accumulate wealth.

Peasant Inequality

What can historical sociologists who want to study inequality before the twentieth century do to overcome limited data and the difficulties of comparing different property systems?

First, they can present the dynamics of inequality in different social systems. Teodor Shanin (1972) offers a model of how to do that. He analyzed changes in the size of peasant landholdings in Russia in the decades leading up to the 1917 Revolution. Because Russia remained largely a peasant society until so late, and since by the early twentieth century it already had good records of landholdings, Shanin is able to give us the best understanding we have of peasant mobility, which after all is how the vast majority of families gained and lost standing in most human societies for most of human history.

Shanin finds that marriages, numbers of children, and economic vicissitudes created cyclical mobility. Children from relatively well-off peasant households partitioned off and created new families with smaller holdings, while other families managed to accumulate larger holdings. However, Shanin finds that peasant families were not just passive victims of demographic and economic forces. Families came together into communes, which were active in allocating land in ways that made holdings more egalitarian, and which pushed back against noble demands for higher rents and state demands for taxes, even as capitalist markets created new sources of peasant inequality. Those dynamics were transformed by the 1917 Revolution. Communes took charge of the redistribution of noble and rich peasant lands, strengthening middle peasants and isolating kulaks. This division among peasants undermined resistance to Stalin's demands for collectivization.

The distribution of wealth affects the distribution of power, and vice versa. Stated at such a general level, it is a claim that can be, and has been, made by Marx, Weber, and numerous other sociologists. However, the goal is to develop theories that can explain the dynamics of the interaction between wealth and power. Shanin accomplishes that for Russia before and after the 1917 Revolution, showing how the interaction between wealth and power on the small scale of peasant villages operated under a czarist and then a Soviet regime. Similarly, Rebecca Jean Emigh (2009) shows how the economic and political interventions of Florentine nobles and merchants affected the distribution of peasant landholdings and local power relations in the countryside around Renaissance Florence.

Emigh's goal is not to explain Florentine politics. Instead, she wants to explain why, even though conditions seemed ripe for capitalist development, economic development in the Tuscan countryside was aborted. Florentines' involvement in rural regions, which formed part of their capitalist strategies, paradoxically undermined further, more widespread capitalist development because it removed rural inhabitants, the majority of the population at that time, from participation in capitalist markets. They were much poorer than Florentines, and thus unable to compete effectively in markets with them. Tuscan smallholders, like Shanin's peasants, were stratified by demographic forces. Demographic patterns connected them to local markets in the rural regions, because they used local markets and property devolution practices to arrange household agricultural production in light of their own demographic configurations, such as family size and age. But when Florentine capitalists then entered these local markets and began buying land, they destroyed local institutions, pulling the smallholders out of markets instead of intensifying their participation in them. Smallholders simply could not compete with the wealth of Florentines in the land market, so the latter were able to consolidate landholdings by buying from rural inhabitants, which blocked the embryonic transition to capitalism in rural Tuscany. This, in turn, changed the stratification system. Tuscan sharecroppers became stratified by their network ties to landlords more than by demographic forces.

Emigh, like Shanin, examines a single case. However, her work is comparative in conception. She is well known among historical sociologists for developing "case methodology" (1997a), which uses single cases that contradict predicted outcomes to challenge existing models and propose revisions or new theories. Shanin, although he does not couch it in that way, also is trying to explain a negative: the absence of forceful resistance to Soviet collectivization. For both Shanin and Emigh, the first step in their analysis is to construct a model of the dynamics of inequality and mobility – in Russian peasant communities and among Tuscan smallholders and sharecroppers, respectively. Those models can then explain negative outcomes: the absence of capitalist development in Tuscany and the absence of forceful resistance by kulaks to Soviet expropriations of their lands.

The lesson we can take away from both Shanin and Emigh's important books is that we need to immerse ourselves in the historical specifics of a case (or of multiple cases) if we actually want to see how inequality is produced and how it changes over time. There never is a simple relationship between power and wealth. Rather, the structure of each society shapes the relationship, which in turn is mediated by demographics, economic cycles, and often other dynamics as well. General theories of power might sensitize us to factors we need to examine, but they cannot automatically be used to get at the interaction of power and wealth in a particular time and place.

Nor are studies of peasants sufficient to give a full picture of inequality in agrarian societies. Inequality varies among strata, as well as between societies and historical eras. That is why Emigh analyzes patterns of wealth accumulation among Florentine elites as well as among peasants, since it is the two systems of stratification together that help explain the contraction of Tuscan capitalism. Thus, to understand the dynamics of any peasant society, we need to examine the top few percent that were aristocrats and high religious officials in addition to the 90 percent who were peasants. Of course, there was some variation in the percentages of each society who were peasants and aristocrats. However, until the development of large-scale markets, farmers (who could be slaves, peasants, or independent farmers) were close to 90 percent in almost all societies, while the elite ranged from 1 to 3 percent, with the remaining tenth or less of the population comprised of lesser aristocrats, officials, merchants, artisans, and various sorts of proto-professionals (such as scribes, doctors, and teachers). These middle strata became significant only in the past few centuries. We will examine how sociologists study the rise and dynamics of the middle class in the last part of this chapter.

Elites and Inequality

There is almost no historical sociology that looks at the dynamics of inequality among nobles. That is a pity, because there was huge variation in the wealth and power of aristocrats. The poorest nobles had incomes of four to ten times that of the better-off peasants, while great nobles and monarchs (and high religious officials) had incomes hundreds to tens of thousands of times that of peasants. Historical studies of the dynamics of mobility among aristocratic families are almost non-existent. Historians have written many studies of individual noble families, and documented how they made or lost their wealth, but those case studies have not been used to draw broad conclusions.

The British historian Lawrence Stone (1965; Stone and Stone 1984) is exemplary, and unusual, because he explored how political changes at the national level (English kings' ability to disarm great nobles) degraded the abilities of nobles to collect revenues from their estates and from political offices while increasing their obligations to offer hospitality to fellow nobles and lesser gentleman, creating a financial crises for that elite. Stone connects aristocrats' financial pressures to their role in the English Civil War, just as Bearman and Deane (1992) find that reduced opportunities for merchants, tradesman, and skilled craftsmen in early seventeenth-century England radicalized those middle strata. Bearman and Deane use their careful reconstruction of fathers' and sons' occupations in Norfolk to trace mobility across generations and then link shifts in opportunities to political allegiances and actions.

Taken together, Stone's study of changes in aristocratic stratification and Bearman and Deane's examination of mobility in the middle class identify a mechanism that can explain political motivations and actions. They show how blocked mobility or decline had consequences for the national polity as well as for the individuals or families that are the focus of most work on inequality. Stone goes further in identifying and tracing the political causes of inequality.

Norbert Elias offers a different sort of model ([1969] 1983). He does not present any quantitative data on nobles' wealth or on whether it increased or decreased over time. Like Stone, he begins with aristocrats' disarming by kings and their relegation to passive lives as hangers-on at royal courts. Elias examines the codes of behavior that nobles developed at court and discusses how court manners affected behavior in the broader society, and also how those codes limited nobles' ability to form political alliances against monarchs. He marshals qualitative evidence to argue that nobles became poorer as they lost political power. (Stone, while also building an argument largely on qualitative evidence, made an effort to amass and analyze what quantitative data he could find for England.) Elias is not concerned with tracking changes in inequality but rather proceeds directly from his assertion of aristocrats' material decline to the cultural and political consequences of that decline. His work alerts us to the value of non-quantitative and cultural evidence (we will have more to say about Elias in chapter 8), and he reminds us that we should attempt to track changes in inequality not just for themselves but for what they can tell us about how they affect the capacities of declining strata to control their social relations and to influence the entire society.

Middle Classes

The most significant change in stratification over the past several centuries has been the enormous increase in middle strata. Today peasants/farmers are a minority in most societies, and a tiny minority in advanced industrial societies. They have been supplanted first by wage laborers and increasingly by middle classes that are marked by at least a modest degree of professional or craft qualifications and/or control over their own work and/or direct sale of their own products or services to customers. Much of the individual mobility tracked by sociologists and economists has little to do with changes in the personal characteristics of workers, and is mainly the result of the massive shift of jobs from the countryside to cities and suburbs, and from farms to factories and then to offices.

The economist Simon Kuznets (1955) argued that, initially, industrialization and the move to cities increased relative inequality – i.e., factory owners benefited from the low wages they could pay to farmers arriving in cities, while food prices and farm incomes remained low as mechanization increased food supply. Later, inequality would diminish as the supply of peasants available to migrate to cities and undercut existing workers' wages declined. The problem with Kuznets's theory is similar to the criticisms of modernization theory we saw in chapter 2: both present a single path of development and are unable to account for, because they do not acknowledge, the possibility of divergent outcomes. The only thing that varies in either model is the speed of the transition. For Kuznets, countries with high levels of inequality have yet to travel past the peak of migration from the countryside. His model has no way of accounting for increases in inequality in industrialized countries of the sort that has occurred in the US since the 1980s.

One way to get at the actual mechanisms that generate and change inequality within middle classes and in relation to elites is to examine moments of fundamental transformation. That is what Emigh did for a (failed) transition to capitalism and Shanin for the transition to socialism. Another such moment is the end of state socialism and the transition to various forms of market capitalism in Eastern Europe after 1989. Ivan Szelenyi and his collaborators (Eyal, Szelenyi, and Townsley 1998; King and Szelenyi 2004) provide a fruitful approach to explaining changes in social systems and their effects on inequality.

Szelenyi and his colleagues are interested in explaining mobility: they want to trace how different Eastern European elites gained or lost income and social position in the 1980s and 1990s, both before and after regime changes. They also want to explain why certain elites fared better than others within each country and the differences among countries. How did they go about gathering data and constructing explanations?

First, they drew up three lists of the elites in each Eastern European country in the years before and after 1989. One list is of pre-1989 "nomenklatura" – the people who held positions in government or in state-owned enterprises that were at such a high level they needed to be approved for those positions by "some organ of the Central Committee of the Communist Party" (Eyal, Szelenyi, and Townsley 1998, p. 201). The second list is of "cultural and political elites" in 1993. These are people who held high positions in post-communist governments. The third list is of economic elites, the CEOs of the 3,000 largest firms in each country in 1993.

The lists allow Szelenyi et al. to trace what happened to the communist-era elites. Did they maintain their positions in the new governments and privatized firms, or did they fall into the middle class? The second and third lists are used to identify the characteristics of the people who rose into elite positions after 1989. Szelenyi and his collaborators then surveyed samples of all three lists.

The lists and surveys give empirical rigor to Szelenyi et al.'s analyses of the transition in each country. They are able to specify the characteristics of the people who rose and fell between the middle class and elite in each country. They could have used the data to build a status attainment model, showing the role of education, family background, previous job, age, gender, ethnicity, and other factors in determining mobility. In fact, they do find that these factors mattered for individuals. However, characteristics that were helpful for upward mobility in some countries were drawbacks in others, and vice versa.

How do Szelenyi and his colleagues explain cross-national differences in mobility? They integrate political factors into their model, but in an even more sophisticated and nuanced way than Stone or Bearman and Deane, whom we examined earlier in this chapter. Szelenyi et al. need a more complex model since they are trying to explain differences among a number of cases, while Stone and Bearman and Deane examined England alone. However, Szelenyi's sophistication is more than just accounting for differences across cases; he identifies causal interaction between the ambitions and ideologies of individual members of the elite and political events that undermined state socialism and shaped the new regimes.

King and Szelenyi (2004) find splits within the communist-era nomenklatura: those who attempted to rise from middle strata but were blocked by higher-level party officials sought other avenues of mobility in the partially privatized economic sector that emerged under communism. To the extent that private enterprise offered higher incomes than party positions, lower-level party officials entered into business, creating a split between them and party elites and also with middle strata who continued to devote their efforts to maintaining or advancing their careers within the party. In this way, technocrats in the Eastern European parties who saw their careers and hopes for reform blocked found a new path to advance themselves and to challenge state socialism in the emerging private sector, which is why they abandoned state socialism and became the leading edge of capitalist enterprise.

Mobility, and the generation of inequality, is a complex and contingent process in Szelenyi et al.'s analyses. What any individual is trying to achieve changes as the political environment shifts. Where once party position was the determinant of material rewards, power, and prestige, the opening of a private sector created both a new path to move upward and a new set of rewards: money without power, and with less prestige than came from party position. As party rule unraveled, the prestige of a position in the nomenklatura declined, as did the security of such positions and the opportunities to rise further.

As the paths to mobility changed, the shifting individual calculations of party members and middle strata coalesced to create new bases of opposition to state socialism. "It was indeed the new technocratic elite rather than the dissident intellectuals who began to call for the second economic reform" in the 1980s (King and Szelenyi 2004, p 120). The calculations and sensibilities of technocrats, who were in semi-privatized state firms and who hoped to find opportunities if those firms were further privatized, became a political force. The technocrats challenged the legitimacy of party rule. This did not happen uniformly across Eastern Europe, as Eyal, Szelenyi, and Townsley show. In the countries where economic liberalization had proceeded further in the 1960s and 1970s, the technocratic elite was larger and had a more realistic chance of benefiting from a push for further liberalization. That is why the political shift was mainly internally driven in Hungary and Poland, while elsewhere in Eastern Europe party rule and state socialism collapsed suddenly in 1989 as the Soviet Union under Gorbachev withdrew support for old-line party regimes and pressed for rapid reform.

The way in which state socialism was undone shaped opportunities for mobility and the structures of inequality after 1989. Members of middle strata were more likely to benefit from the expansion of already liberalized economies in Hungary and Poland than elsewhere in Eastern Europe. Paths upward in the rest of Eastern Europe and Russia were much more fragmented in the absence of an already existing substantial and viable private sector. "Not only did the technocracy fail to depose the bureaucratic elite in Russia, it is questionable if the distinction between technocracy and bureaucracy holds for Russia at all" (Eyal, Szelenyi, and Townsley 1998, p. 167). Eyal et al. find that the Eastern European states were closer to this Russian reality than to the pattern of Hungary and Poland, and therefore party officials in the East enjoyed more opportunity to engage in "political capitalism," enriching themselves by taking ownership of state assets rather than creating new enterprises, alone or in cooperation with investors from Western Europe. Elites in Eastern Europe therefore practiced a different politics as well: seeking to strengthen the states in which they held positions and from which they could profit.

Szelenyi and his colleagues are able to account for variation in inequality across countries and over a decade of rapid structural change. To use Tilly's terminology, they show how changes in state policies created opportunities for nomenklatura at the middle and upper levels to engage in new forms of exploitation and hoarding, just as the conquest of the Tuscan countryside did for Emigh's Florentine elite and the 1917 Revolution did briefly for middle peasants until Stalin's collectivization. While Szelenyi et al. are able to identify the characteristics of those who benefited from those opportunities (and those who could not and therefore fell into lower strata), their main achievement is to show how individual efforts concatenated into pressures on the state and on enterprises and produced further change in the structure of opportunities. Their work, although it borrows aspects of status attainment methodology and succeeds in answering the sorts of questions posed by status attainment scholars, is fully historical because it shows how the criteria of stratification, the individual qualities recognized by the stratification system, and the structures that determine the size and distribution of rewards interacted with one another to determine the magnitude, direction, and timing of change. Szelenyi et al. explain how politics mattered for the drastic increase in inequality that occurred in the former Soviet bloc. Their approach, and those of Shanin and Emigh, as well as Tilly's theoretical framework, offers models of how to construct an historical explanation for the increase in inequality in the US and elsewhere in recent decades. These historical sociologists recognize what status attainment researchers ignore: that inequality is created mainly by large political processes and changes mostly during moments of transition. Historical sociology is sensitive to temporal and geographic differences rather than assuming a universal theory based on the US experience. Inequality affects individuals, but it is created by large social forces that manifest differently in each historical era.

7
Gender and the Family

Social actors through most of human history identified themselves as members of families or kin groups rather than as individuals. As Wally Seccombe (1992, p. 23), puts it: "People make enormous sacrifices to safeguard their families' continuity, honour and living standards . . . Within the domestic circle, individuals still act in self-interested ways, but they are severely constrained by their position in the family and the need to preserve close ties" with family members. For that reason, sociological and historical analyses are incomplete to the extent that they fail to show how familial identities affected social actors' loyalties, interests, and calculations. This is a matter not just of making women subjects of study in themselves, but also of recognizing the need to incorporate gender and family dynamics in building more accurate explanations of historical change in all domains, such as state formation, inequality, and governmental policies. As in previous chapters, we will see how gender and family can best be studied historically, and employed in historical sociological explanation, by examining a few exemplary works.

Historical demographers have focused their research on couples' decisions to marry and have children, seeking to identify factors that explain temporal and geographic differences in fertility rates. Most of this scholarship is structured to explain what individuals such as Kingsley Davis

(1955), John Hajnal (1965), and Lutz Berkner (1978) present as personal choices, much like status attainment researchers concentrate on individual characteristics to explain income differences. These authors compare societies in which couples form nuclear families (and hence need to wait until they can accumulate enough resources to start their own households before marrying and having children) with societies in which young couples can marry and have children at an earlier age, since they can draw on the extended family with whom they live for support. They show how inheritance and household patterns come together to determine access to land and create stable demographic patterns.[17] This approach, like status attainment research, tends to examine continuities in individual and familial practices in isolation from national and local economic and political forces that disrupt and transform demographic and familial patterns, but which also are influenced by gender and family.

Historian Lawrence Stone's *The Family, Sex and Marriage in England, 1500–1800* (1977) is an early example of an effort to trace, in a single country over centuries, changes in family structure and in the cultural expectations and actual practices of elites and middle classes toward marital relations and childrearing. Stone explains those changes in terms of shifts in the state's capacity to intervene in kin groups and families and what he sees as oscillations between liberalism and repression. More recently, Wally Seccombe (1992) looks at the interaction between temporal change within a family – when its members "achieve a livelihood," acquire space (land and/or a home), start a family, marry, bear and raise children, and provide for their elderly parents (p. 25) – and transformations in the mode of production. He traces how peasants, as families and as localized and regional classes, adjusted their fertility and altered their family structure in an effort to challenge or mitigate their exploitation by landlords. Thus, repeated efforts to maximize rather than reduce fertility and the transition from extended (stem) to nuclear families are, in Seccombe's analysis, the result of openings that wage labor created for younger members of stem families to escape manorial constraints, and for their elders to gain leverage against landlords.

Seccombe's focus complements Shanin's, which we examined in the previous chapter. Shanin took family size as a given, describing but not explaining changes in fertility so that he could explore how practices within families or localities amalgamated into a political force that affected politics on a large scale. Seccombe, in contrast, explains how changes in the mode of production, above all the rise of wage labor in the centuries of putting out and proto-industry, affected family size and weakened extended families. However, his focus on the interaction between the family and mode of production bypasses casualty at the intermediate political level. Unlike Shanin, Seccombe does not show how family practices affected the political conflicts that shaped and propelled transformations in the mode of production. Yet, in a subsequent volume (1993) on the industrial revolution, he does explain how families came to make political demands for birth control. In so doing, Seccombe constructs a causal model for the emergence of widespread effective birth control and the subsequent sharp decline in fertility in a few and then in more, though not all, regions of the world, a transition described but not explained by Goran Therborn (2004) in his global history of twentieth-century family types.

Seccombe (1993) notes that effective birth control requires the participation of both partners. Drawing on diaries, letters, and rare government and private surveys from nineteenth-century Europe, he shows that women were eager to limit the size of their families decades before men joined them in that desire. Women were frustrated in their efforts by husbands, who refused to practice coitus interruptus, engage in non-genital sex, or use condoms, and hindered both by physicians, who refused to discuss effective methods of birth control, and by governments, which sought to increase birth rates to provide laborers, tax payers, and soldiers. Yet, by the early twentieth century, the working class in much of Western Europe was practicing birth control effectively enough to reduce the birth rate significantly. How did that happen?

Seccombe identifies factors that recast the outlooks and practices of working-class families. States and elites were critical. Elite couples limited their fertility in the nineteenth century, showing working-class men and women that it was possible to do so, that the number of children was not a matter of fate. Seccombe supports that hypothesis with narrative evidence, quoting liberally from working-class diaries and letters. Second, working-class couples' economic calculus changed. As states succeeded in forcing parents to keep their children in school for more and more years, parents could no longer profit from sending their children out to work. Children thus were transformed from economic assets that began paying a return at age eight or ten into expenses that continued until age twelve or fourteen, shortly before they left home. Although states did not institute mass schooling in an effort to reduce the birth rate, that was the effect it had.

Once working-class couples agreed on the desirability of limiting their families, birth control became a political issue. Therborn noted that – but did not explain why – governments in Scandinavia and then a few other nations adopted policies that made birth control and fertility reduction easier for their citizens. Seccombe answers that government programs to provide, or legalize access to, birth control were a response to popular pressure. Thus, Scandinavian governments were progressive on birth control and women's rights because their earlier policies of instituting mass education changed the structure of the economy, transformed family dynamics, and led working-class voters to put birth control on the political agenda.

Seccombe's work on European families during the Industrial Revolution shows how a rich analysis of documents from everyday family life can be used to explore the dynamic interaction between macro-change in the economy and structural change in the family. He suggests, but does not fully work out, how families became political actors, pressuring states and parties to respond to their concerns and to meet their demands. Julia Adams (2005) focuses her attention on precisely that problem. She is concerned with analyzing how elite families protected and advanced their interests and the effects of those efforts on the structures and trajectories of states. Adams links family to state, as Emigh, whom we examined above, ties family to capitalist dynamics.

Adams, following Weber, sees patrimonial rule as a "state [in which] political power and administration are considered the ruler's 'personal property'" (2005, p. 16). Adams goes beyond Weber, and brings gender and family into the analysis, by showing that patriarchs in early modern Europe were not just individuals acting to appropriate state property and power for their personal benefit. "Patriarchy is broader than [Seccombe's (1992)] idea of a family form characterized by male headship" (pp. 31–2). Instead, patriarchs were heads of households that had complex and shifting internal relations that affected their ability to vie for state power or to amass wealth.

Adams, like Seccombe, looks at the internal dynamics of early modern families, but she incorporates into her analysis dimensions Seccombe and others slight. She focuses on relations between parents and children, and especially the differential statuses and positions of eldest sons, younger sons, and daughters. In part, Adams is able to get at the relations among siblings because they matter for the ambitions of elite families in ways that they did not for the peasant and proletarian families Seccombe studies (although differences between siblings are a crucial element in shaping intergenerational mobility in Shanin's model).

Patriarchal families did not pursue their interests in isolation. They constantly bumped up against other such families that were competing for political power and economic advantage. The patrimonial states of early modern Europe did not have defined external borders. Nor were their institutions clearly differentiated: armies, courts, tax collectors, public works, churches – all the state-like tasks undertaken by these proto-states – were performed by competing and overlapping organizations which were parts of patriarchal families. Early modern states were little more than amalgamations of the claims and capacities of elite families. Adams, by analyzing how these families sought to guard their interests on such uncertain and shifting terrains, shows that the dynamics of state formation owed as much to competition among families as it did to the sort of competition among rulers that Tilly's model (which we examined in chapter 5) emphasizes.

Adams's focus on the internal relations of patriarchal elite families, and on their members' interactions, reveals an aspect of state formation ignored by other scholars who fail to examine (or often even to recognize) familial and gender dynamics. Adams finds that elite families often did not fight each other for power and privilege. Rather, they compromised, drawing up contracts and pacts to divide state revenues and offices, and later international trade routes and colonial lands and offices. Adams reaches this understanding through an extended case study of the Netherlands, which pioneered this method of familial compromise, and thereby pushed past its geopolitical rivals to build one of the leading military powers of the seventeenth century and to create a colonial empire and trading network that allowed the Dutch to achieve economic hegemony in Europe for decades. Adams's attention to familial dynamics, and her identification of patriarchs as the key political actors in early modern Europe, allows her to see, as previous historians and sociologists did not, the pioneering path of the Netherlands toward state formation. Previous scholars, who focused on individual actors rather than families, therefore present a less complete picture of the process of state formation and global expansion.

Adams's book illuminates family dynamics, but her goal is different from that of Seccombe, who is interested primarily in tracing and explaining changes in family forms over time. Adams's patrimonial families endure, and their internal structure and dynamics are relatively stable in the centuries she examines. Her goal is instead to explain state formation. Mounira Charrad (2001) takes a different though complementary approach: her aim is to explain the different policies on women's rights adopted in post-colonial Tunisia, Algeria, and Morocco.

Charrad poses a clear comparative problem: Why did the newly independent former French colonies of Tunisia, Algeria, and Morocco "follow markedly different paths with respect to family law"? (2001, p. 2). She notes that the three countries had fundamental similarities: all had been French colonies, were Muslim, and were neighbors in the Maghreb of northwestern Africa. In none of the

three "was there a broad-based, grassroots women's movement demanding the expansion of women's rights in the
1950s." Instead, "actions of family law came 'from the
top'" (ibid.). The new Tunisian state promulgated laws
that banned polygamy, gave husbands and wives equal
rights in filing for divorce, and expanded mothers' custody
rights and daughters' inheritance rights. At the same time,
Moroccan law codified Islamic practices that discriminated
against women in divorce, custody, and inheritance. Algerian
"family law became caught in paralyzing gridlock between
reformist and conservative tendencies for more than two
decades after independence in 1962. During that time reform
plans aborted repeatedly until a conservative family code
faithful to Islamic law was promulgated in 1984" (ibid.,
p. 1).

Charrad explains the different outcomes in the three
countries by looking at the relationship between the state
and tribes as it changed from the pre-colonial to the colonial and then the post-independence era. Tribes are amalgamations of extended kin groups that came together to
protect land rights and to block demands by pre-colonial
states for taxes. The dynamics of tribes therefore are somewhat different than those of the patriarchal families Adams
studies in that they included multiple patriarchs of the
numerous extended families within each tribe. Charrad does
not focus her attention on those internal dynamics in the
way that Adams or Seccombe do. Instead, she compares
state–tribe relations across the three societies. Thus, in the
pre-colonial era, Tunisia's relatively strong state was able
to impose some degree of uniformity on family and property law in the tribes, while the weak Algerian state did
not attempt any such control, allowing each tribe to rule
itself. In Morocco the weak state was more ambitious
and locked in perpetual and inconclusive struggle with
the tribes.

French colonialism altered state–tribe relations in each
country. Colonization was, in Sewell (1996) and Abrams's
(1982) terms, eventful, disrupting chronic and inconclusive
conflicts and transforming tribal and national social structures, as were the later struggles for independence in the
three countries. The French and later the independence

movements allied with or sought to weaken tribes as part of strategies to achieve and maintain political power. Nationalist groups fought with one another as well as with the French. Tribes were potentially decisive, and factions of the independence movements had to decide what stance to adopt on family law to win tribes' allegiance, and whether that alliance could be justified strategically or ideologically to other supporters. Thus, the Moroccan king allied with tribes to undercut both the French and urban nationalists. Algeria's long and brutal struggle against the French ended with a factionalized independent state divided between secular urban and rural tribal power blocs. The conflict took over twenty years to resolve. Finally, in 1984, the government passed a conservative family law in order to strengthen the support of rural tribes. Urban, educated women's resistance to previous conservative drafts of the law was overcome by state repression. Neither colonization nor the independence struggle had weakened tribes enough, or strengthened women as a political force sufficiently, to alter the ultimate outcome. Tunisian political centralization in the pre-colonial era carried over into the struggle for independence, which was urban-dominated and centered on a single nationalist party. There was a rural, Islamist faction in the independence movement, but it was overwhelmed (in part with the help of the French, who preferred to deal with a secular rather than a pan-Arab Islamist independent regime). The liberal family law reflected the weakening of tribes under French colonialism and the urban political base and centralizing interests of the new post-independence Tunisian government.

Charrad traces regime change through the colonial and independence eras to explain the sort of family law each regime promulgated. But her picture of the polity is given complexity and precision by her recognition of the key role played by patriarchal tribes in all three countries, just as Adams allows us better to understand state formation by recognizing the role of patriarchal elite families. For Charrad, family law and state power, and for Adams the very structure and capacity of the state, are shaped by patriarchal family and tribal dynamics respectively.

Nuclear families of the modern age are actors upon, as well as recipients of, state programs and policies. How that causal interaction works and its effects over time form the subject of a debate between Gøsta Esping-Andersen (whose work on welfare states we examined in chapter 5) and Ann Orloff and her collaborators. Orloff (1993) accurately criticizes Esping-Andersen (1990) for slighting the ways in which different social welfare regimes affect gender relations, reinforcing or challenging men's power within the family. For example, Esping-Andersen does not attempt to explain differences among countries in the provision of childcare, which plays a greater role than the overall level of social benefits in determining women's participation in the labor force, nor does he address women's role in the 'private' (i.e., non-state) provision of social goods and services through their unpaid labor. Orloff argues further that women often have different political positions on welfare policies because they are affected by them differently than are men. Even within a single type of welfare regime such as the Scandinavian social democratic system, differences in family policies, and variations in family relations and women's access to the labor market, can produce different consequences for women's income, well-being, and autonomy across countries.

While gender politics was absent from Esping-Andersen (1990), in a subsequent volume Esping-Andersen (1999) addresses some of the issues Orloff raised. He goes well beyond his earlier book in analyzing how policies in each of the three types of social welfare system affects women's material circumstances and social citizenship. He does not examine what openings each regime provides for women's political activity, or how women's political mobilization affects the total constellation of power in a society and therefore future opportunities to preserve or expand the welfare state regimes. As a result, his analysis is static. There is little historical dynamic. Once the type of social welfare regime is set, it has a constant effect on gender relations and women's social position. Women in both Esping-Andersen's books are passive recipients of government programs. They are not political actors, and as a result his model fails to account for changes in gender relations or in social programs that specifically affect women, except as part of overall changes in the social welfare regime.

O'Connor, Orloff, and Shaver (1999) provide a way to explain change in gender relations in both the family and state over time. They examine how state policies affect women in three realms: the labor market, cash transfers, and reproductive rights. Rather than look at cases from each type of social welfare regime, they compare four liberal regimes (the US, Canada, Australia, and Britain). In that way they can both focus on how differences in gender relations and power affect politics and policy and avoid the confounding effects of the very different dynamics in conservative and social democratic welfare regimes. Potentially, other scholars could perform a similar analysis for the other two types of regime.

Changes in social welfare policies transform politics: Esping-Andersen recognizes that at the level of classes, unions, and parties, but not for gender. O'Connor et al., by showing how social welfare affects and is affected by gender relations, provide a method for developing an historical analysis of how women's role in social welfare politics changes over time. They make mention of the rising force of market liberalism or neoconservatism over recent decades, and note that resistance to it is built and sustained in very different ways by women and allied men who mobilize on gender issues than it is by the groups Esping-Andersen and others identify as most active on non-gender social issues. They find that, in the US and Canada, women mobilize to make claims based on legal claims to equal rights, such as demanding equal pay for equal work in the private sector, while women in Australia and Britain demand inclusion in existing programs that confer social benefits initially won by unions and other class-based organizations.

Orloff and her colleagues, like Charrad, Adams, and Seccombe, recognize that gender and family can't be subsumed within class or other categories. Nor can family dynamics be studied in isolation. If we want to engage in writing historical sociology of gender and the family, our goal must be, as it is in different and at times incomplete ways for these scholars, to trace the interactions of familial, economic, and political structures, and to identify the places and moments when actors are able to make eventful changes that reconfigure the ground for further conflict and change. The best works recognize that often openings for further action narrow in the various family forms, social welfare regimes, states, and economic structures created by previous conflicts.

8
Culture

Historical sociologists – indeed, all sociologists – need to figure out how social actors make sense of themselves and of what they do. For some historical sociologists, understanding actors' perceptions is a worthy topic of study in itself. For others it is necessary for explaining the origins of capitalism, the course and outcomes of revolutions, the varying ways in which imperialists seek to rule their subjects, or whatever is their subject of interest. In the last chapter we saw that the acknowledgment and careful study of how individuals identify themselves as parts of families and lineages is essential to understanding the origins of states or variations across countries and over time in social welfare policies.

Adams, Clemens, and Orloff (2005), in a highly influential essay, argue that US historical sociology in the last twenty years has entered what they describe as a "third wave" which has been concerned much more with culture than either of the two previous waves of scholarship. In their analysis, the first wave was concerned with the origins of the modern world. The founding fathers, Marx, Weber, Durkheim, and their successors, dealt with the largest of questions, as we saw in chapter 1. While the big three certainly addressed culture, it was at such a grand, macro-level that they didn't provide much basis for concrete studies of change at actual historical moments, and when they tried to use grand theory they often ended up distorting the actual history, as Weber did in his *Protestant Ethic*. Nor were Marx, Weber, and Durkheim of much help in explaining differences across space or over time at a more fine-grained level than the epochal transformations about which they wrote. We saw the limits of such grand theorizing in chapter 2 when we critiqued the limitations of Eisenstadt's (1968) efforts to "search for equivalents of the Protestant ethic in non-Western societies." Similarly, modernization theory tried to press all countries' histories of the last few centuries into a single transformation, albeit at different speeds, from traditional to modern societies.

Adams et al. (2005) accurately describe the second wave as a reaction to the simplifications and overgeneralizations of modernization theory. The leaders of that wave, most notably Theda Skocpol and Charles Tilly, sought to bring scientific rigor to historical sociology by formulating problems in terms of social structural change that could be carefully specified, and by trying to test Marxist and Weberian theories (and the particular blends of those and other perspectives developed by each second-wave author) across a range of problems, locales, and time periods.

Second-wave historical sociologists' emphasis on structure had the, somewhat unintended, effect of slighting culture. As a result, "the paradigm that guided second-wave work proved unable to deal with a whole series of epochal transformations": the new social movements, "feminism, gay liberation, ongoing rebellions among post-colonials and racial and ethnic minorities" and the rise of "feminist theory, post-colonial theory, queer theory, and critical race studies" (Adams et al. 2005, p. 29). Those intellectual challenges to Marxism and to Marxist-inspired second-wave historical sociology were compounded in Adams, Clemens, and Orloff's view by the actual collapse of socialist regimes in 1989 and "the subsequent revival of liberalism, the vagaries of globalization, [and] fundamental challenges to the order of nation-states" (ibid.).[18]

Adams and her colleagues in their essay, and also in their own historical work, offer a range of suggestions as to how culturally informed historical analysis can overcome the limitations of second-wave structural analysis to address the social movements and historical transformations of recent decades. Orloff's (1993; and O'Connor, Orloff, and Shaver 1999) own work on the role of gender and family in shaping the content and implementation of social benefits, which we examined in the previous chapter, is an example of how culturally informed historical sociology can speak to the impact of new social movements on the state. Similarly, Adams's (2005) work, also examined in chapter 7, which traced the causal interactions between culture and structure in the seventeenth century, offers a model of how such an analysis could be used to explain recent as well as long-ago epochal transformations, as does George Steinmetz (2007, 2008) whose work on German colonialism we discussed in chapter 4. Philip Gorski (2003), Eiko Ikegami (1995), and Mary Fulbrook (1983), whom we encountered in chapter 2, present nuanced understandings of religion and its multifaceted and indirect effect on capitalist development and state formation.

Adams et al.'s essay is focused mainly on the US, and therefore its history of the role of culture in historical sociology slights many of the significant contributions of non-Americans and also of much of the work by historians that could guide both a culturalist historical sociology of institutions and the study of historical change in cultural practices and a sociology of ideas. The mainly French "history of mentalities," which began in the 1960s and was heavily influenced by the translation of Mikhail Bakhtin's *Rabelais and his World* ([submitted as a dissertation in the Soviet Union in 1940, and published in its final form in Russian and French in 1965] 1968), offers a model of how to study culture historically. Bakhtin addresses a vast subject: the emergence and development of class society. He does so by analyzing with great specificity Rabelais' novels *Gargantua* and *Pantagruel*, first published in the 1530s. Bakhtin argues that these works provide a window into pre-class society, which he saw as being finally suppressed just when Rabelais wrote. He mines the novels for clues as to how ordinary people still were able to challenge their rulers. The elements of carnival and grotesque in the novels were, in Bakhtin's analysis, evidence of actual rituals

and practices that challenged and reversed the class hierarchy that was finally being locked into place in the Renaissance centuries.

Bakhtin was so influential above all because he pointed
scholars to unusual documents, such as novels, and to
innovative techniques for drawing historical evidence from
them, to get at how otherwise anonymous common people
lived and thought. His work influenced historians and
(mainly European) social scientists to look to literature,
police records, transcripts of inquisition trials, paintings,
and other artifacts in new ways for clues as to how people
thought as well as of their material circumstances. Rabelais'
novels contained evidence of an alternative social order
that Bakhtin argues actually existed in the late medieval
and Renaissance eras and competed in towns and villages,
on manors, and in armies for institutional and cultural
dominance.

Culture, for Bakhtin, is simultaneously a way of creating
social relations capable of challenging authority and hierarchy and of envisioning an alternative order. Thus, medieval
carnival drew people together to mock and also substantively
to challenge the powerful, while presenting a non-hierarchical
society which carnival participants actually could create.
That is why, Bakhtin asserts, "carnival does not know foot-
lights" ([1965] 1968, p. 7). The power of the carnival was
that it was not a fantasy to be watched or a satire to be
enjoyed. Rather, it was a plausible alternative that participants had it in their power to create.

Bakhtin shows that, once class society became irreversibly
cemented into place in early modern Europe, the meaning
of carnival, as an event and as a trope in literature, was
transformed. The grotesque imagery of actual carnival and
of Rabelais' novels changed from being a representation and
enactment of the common people's collective capacity to
transform to social world into "a subjective, individualistic
world outlook" ([1965] 1968, p. 36). In the late eighteenth
century, grotesque "acquired a private 'chamber' character
. . . marked by a vivid sense of isolation" (p. 37). "The
images of Romantic grotesque usually express fear of the
world and seek to inspire their reader with this fear. On
the contrary, images of folk culture are absolutely fearless"

(p. 39). Bakhtin finds that twentieth-century grotesque has a "gloomy, terrifying tone . . . In reality gloom is completely alien to the entire development of this world up to the romantic period" (p. 47). He is not just tracing a change in literary form: he is showing that literary and popular imagery changed as actual possibilities of transformative social change were lost in the sixteenth and subsequent centuries.[19]

Norbert Elias ([1939] 1982; [1969] 1983), whom we encountered in chapter 6, is the perfect complement to Bakhtin. Like Bakhtin, he looks at unexpected sources, in his case books of manners, to get at the thoughts as well as the material conditions of otherwise unrecorded actors and their actions. Elias shows, in their increasing attention to courtly manners, the declining political power of aristocrats. He also is able to show how the spread of courtly manners from aristocratic retainers to the middle class was both a measure and a propellant of states' growing capacities to regulate their subjects' lives and to inspire loyalty.

Bakhtin and Elias both make culture their subject to show the opening and closing of possibilities for states and ruling classes to impose order and control over non-elites, and for popular groups to resist those demands and to construct alternatives. In so doing, they also show us ways to study culture on its own terms: through the use of unorthodox sources and methods, and by tracing over time a changing interaction between the ways in which people use culture to think and act, and then to create new cultural forms and to reinterpret past cultural objects and performances. Bakhtin calls this interaction a dialogic process. (He just as well could have labeled it dialectic.) But it is a dialogue not just among literary texts but also between cultural creations and actions that affect social relations. The consequences of those interactions matter and vary over time, which is why both Bakhtin and Elias must be understood to have written historical sociologies of culture.

Sensitivity to time is largely absent from John Meyer's theory of "world culture." His work is a dismal counterpoint to the complexity and temporal nuance of Elias and Bakhtin and of the contemporary scholars Adams et al. highlight. Nevertheless, Meyer's work deserves mention because of the attention it has drawn from so many (mainly US) sociologists.

Meyer et al. (1997) contend that a world culture exists that is characterized by growing consensus around and conformity to norms that view nation-states as the exclusive legitimate organizations for governing territory and embodying national interests. Governments conform to world cultural norms by joining international organizations, signing treaties with one another, and creating national institutions with an ever-higher level of isomorphism. Thus, Meyer's theory contends that governments and their citizens increasingly come to share belief in a world culture that obligates national governments to offer a growing list of rights and services, and which citizens increasingly expect to receive while themselves recognizing their own obligations to a national state which they view as constitutive of their individual identities. According to Meyer, these shared beliefs have given states their legitimacy since the seventeenth century.

At first glance, Meyer et al. seem to be engaged in a similar cultural historical sociology to that of Bakhtin and Elias. Meyer is concerned with tracing change in cultural beliefs and practices over time and with showing how culture guides and limits actors' beliefs and behaviors. However, in practice, Meyer's work is quite different. Unlike Bakhtin and Elias, he is not really looking at change over time. To the extent that Meyer et al. present empirical evidence, it is for the twentieth century and focuses on the adoption by governments of practices and forms borrowed from the most successful states. This "institutional isomorphism" certainly plays a role in explaining why contemporary governments conduct censuses, adopt constitutions, join international agencies, establish ministries of education, and (at least until recently) had a national airline as well as a flag. However, his claim that states' common culture allows for "greater penetration to the level of daily life" (Meyer et al. 1997, p. 146) is not supported by the evidence he presents, which is confined entirely to showing commonalities among state symbols and organizational charts. In any case, his twentieth-century evidence cannot be used to claim that subjects regarded states as legitimate in earlier centuries.

Meyer's approach is not designed to explain differences over time and space or among social groups. Like modernization theory, world culture theory assumes (and selectively studies) data that measure only the speed with which different states are moving toward a common goal. Thus, in Meyer's theory, culture loses any contingency: its content, meaning, and causal role are not subject to change through the actions of, or conflicts among, classes, groups, individuals, or even nations. Not surprisingly, Meyer and his followers therefore have no need, and make no effort, to examine how perceptions and practices of nationalism, citizenship, or social rights vary or change. World culture becomes an ideal type, unlike Elias's courtly culture or Bakhtin's carnival culture, both of which were transformed in the friction generated by differences in how those cultures were perceived and practiced over time and across geographic and social spaces. Elias and Bakhtin, unlike Meyer, are open theoretically and empirically to contingency.

Pascale Casanova ([1999] 2004) offers a fruitful way to study cultural change on a world scale. Her book is a model of how to write an historical sociology of culture. Casanova addresses herself to literary historians and critics, but the method she develops is essentially sociological in that she shows how writers and their works are created and read in a global social system that has grown to encompass formerly autonomous local and national literatures. Her work is historical in that she is concerned with explaining how literary forms changed at different speeds (and in different ways) across geographic space, and with exploring how those differences affect individual literary careers, national literatures, and the dynamics of the world literary system.

Casanova examines how "Writers have to create the conditions under which they can be seen" ([1999] 2004, p. 177). They strive to create those conditions, however, in a world of inequality, a world in which some literatures and some languages have been able to claim a mantle of classicism due to their relatively long histories. French, Italian, and English literatures were the first vernaculars successfully to challenge Latin and with it the dominance of clerical modes of thought and expression.

Casanova shows how the oldest literary traditions are able to define the terms by which new writers are evaluated. Literary worth is set at the centers of the world republic of letters, above all in Paris and London, whose translators and critics decide which peripheral works are worth of translation into French and English, the universal literary languages. Untranslated authors find it impossible to garner attention beyond their home countries. Faulkner, for example, was virtually unknown and unappreciated in the United States until Sartre championed him as a great literary innovator and arranged his translation into French. The Pulitzer and Noble prizes followed. Nabokov first won critical attention in Paris for Russian works translated into French. Gao Xingjian, the first, and so far only, Chinese writer to win the Nobel Prize (in 2000) is a French citizen living in Paris.

Casanova, in true French academic fashion, writes at length (and convincingly) on why Paris rather than London or New York remains the literary capital of the world despite the decline of French literature. The power of Paris's critics and translators, she argues, is augmented by its philosophers of literature – e.g., Foucault, Derrida, and Lacan – even though they are championed mainly in US literature departments. London is a center, but only for writers from its former colonies, and so elicits little translation. New York, she argues, is merely a commercial center, where few foreign authors are translated or read and where true innovation has been replaced by

a composite measure of fictional modernity. Restored to current taste are all the techniques of the popular novel and the serial invented in the nineteenth century: between the covers of a single volume one can find a cloak-and-dagger drama, a detective novel, an adventure story, a tale of economic and political suspense, a travel narrative, a love story, a psychological account, even a novel within the novel, the last a pretext for false self referential erudition. ([1999] 2004, p. 171)

At this point you can insert your own examples of such bastardized writing. Casanova skewers David Lodge and Umberto Eco.

Writers from peripheral lands face the double handicaps of producing works in languages few non-natives read and of being seen as addressing provincial subjects in unsophisticated ways. Much of Casanova's book is devoted to identifying the methods peripheral writers use to develop their national literary spaces and to advance their own careers. "Assimilationists" abandon their own nation and national concerns and language. This strategy usually is unsuccessful; these writers end in obscurity both at home and in the literary center. When successful, such writers become the voice of the periphery in the center – e.g., Naipaul.

Peripheral writers can instead follow a nationalist path and try to raise the prestige of their writing by widening the literary space in their home countries. This strategy, developed by the German writer Johann Herder in the late eighteenth century, begins with the creation of a classical literature in the country's native language. This is accomplished, in part, by translating great foreign works, creating a borrowed classical tradition. The first authors often are conservative in style, and therefore garner little attention abroad. Their sacrifice lays the groundwork for writers who are revolutionary in style: some combine high and vernacular language, such as Mark Twain, who is the inventor of American English as a literary language. (Rabelais accomplished the same feat for French, as Mikhail Bakhtin demonstrated.)

Once a first generation creates national literary resources, subsequent generations have the autonomy to break away from the nationalist model and develop innovative techniques "to transform the signs of cultural, literary, and often economic destitution into literary resources and thus to gain access to the highest modernity" (Casanova [1999] 2004, p. 328). The greatest innovators of the twentieth century (James Joyce, William Faulkner, Samuel Beckett, the authors of the Latin American 'boom' such as García Márquez and Cortázar) redrew the world literary map. Faulkner wrote about "the South . . . a rural and archaic world prey to magical styles of thought and trapped in the closed life of families and villages" (p. 337), but expressed it in modernist and innovative ways, not in realism. He "resolved in an utterly new and masterly fashion the dilemma and difficulties of deprived writers . . ." What Joyce did for "writers from disadvantaged urban backgrounds Faulkner did for the rural" (p. 338).

Casanova's model of an unequal literary world allows her to track paths of literary influence from Faulkner's segregated Mississippi to the Latin American admirers of Castro, Julio Cortázar and Gabriel García Márquez, from Yiddish theatre to Kafka, from James Joyce to the US novelist Henry Roth. Casanova's recognition and analysis of the inequality of literary space and time "has the immediate consequence of rendering obsolete the most common representations of the writer as a pure being, standing outside history" ([1999] 2004, p. 351). It also requires a "new method for interpreting literary texts" (ibid.). Casanova provides that method and in so doing offers a radical new understanding of literary identity and influence. She explains how to locate authors both spatially and temporally within a world system and shows how each author is shaped by, and how a few succeed in transforming, an international system of literary production and consumption.

Casanova's work is historical in that it shows how uneven and incomplete has been the emergence of a world system of literature. The boundaries and dynamics of that system have changed since its first emergence in the Renaissance. As Casanova's rich analysis of writers' dilemmas, choices, and strategies reveals, the world literary system has not expanded evenly, nor can the trajectories of writers' careers or national literatures be understood in terms of isomorphism. Indeed, the innovations in world literature repeatedly came, as Casanova documents, from peripheral languages, literatures, and writers. Literary innovation, which is the dynamic of change in this cultural realm, moved from the periphery to the center, largely the inverse of the top-down processes Elias and Bakhtin found for the spread of courtly manners and the suppression of carnival culture. Yet all three trace complex historical dynamics in which cultural ideas and practices appear as causes and effects at different times and places.

Randall Collins (1998)[20] examines the sources of philosophical creativity throughout the world from ancient times to the present. Unlike Casanova, largely because his cases come mainly from the pre-modern era, Collins finds that great philosophical creativity is highly concentrated in time and place. Our image of Socrates, Plato, and their colleagues discussing ideas face to face in the small city of Athens is an accurate reflection of almost all significant philosophers in world history, who were creative only when and where they were part of dense and small personal networks of fellow thinkers.

Collins builds his analysis on a comprehensive comparison of networks of philosophers in ancient Greece and Rome, China, India, Japan, the Middle East, and modern Europe. He identifies major and secondary philosophers from published histories of philosophy in each of the countries and finds that creativity is spurred by the emotional energy philosophers derive from interactions with fellow thinkers. Collins's philosophers, like Casanova's literary writers, often provoke the greatest intellectual advances by taking positions in opposition to their contemporaries and immediate predecessors. Like Casanova, Collins examines many creative figures to find patterns in how careers are built and how each person goes about positioning him- or herself in relation to peers and esteemed authors from the past. Yet, his picture of philosophical schools is very different from Casanova's of literature in that the philosophers are speaking to other authors within their immediate social circle and to predecessors within their national, religious, or cultural tradition. Casanova's authors, in contrast, have a choice between writing for a national or a global audience, and that choice is central to their careers and the sort of literature they write. Collins's philosophers must write for their local peers if they want to be influential and produce work seen as innovative.

Collins's analysis provides the basis for him to ask and to answer the fundamental historical question about creativity: Why does innovation occur at particular moments in particular places? Part of the dynamic is internal to each philosophical tradition: great philosophers produce students who become major philosophers themselves only if they can challenge their teachers. Yet, as Collins makes clear, major philosophers do not occur in each generation. He found long periods in each area of the world he studied with no significant philosophers. Innovation is sparked by political and economic changes. It is not that philosophers speak directly to those changes (and if they do they are unlikely to become major philosophers themselves). Rather, such societal changes disrupt the material bases of intellectual networks, dividing existing schools of thought and/or unifying marginal and disparate thinkers, thereby producing new intellectual conflicts and innovations in thought.

Philosophical creativity occurred in dialogue with developments in other intellectual disciplines. Religion often was the font of new philosophical concepts and schools. Interactions between Islam, Judaism, and Christianity in the Middle East, and the breakdown of small-scale states in that region, recast networks of philosophers and propelled creativity. In the West, philosophy increasingly overlapped with mathematics, while the two disciplines remained largely separate in the rest of the world. As a result, Western philosophy was transformed by the advent of what Collins describes as "rapid-discovery science." Universities did not necessarily foster philosophical innovation: it depended on the extent to which they were linked to churches and rulers or how their autonomy was structured. Universities today, like those of the Middle Ages, can produce stagnation and scholasticism as well as creativity.

Collins's focus on identifying networks among philosophers and tracing them over time provides the basis for determining how the lodging of members of those networks in universities, in churches, or at royal courts affects the overall cohesion and dynamic of the network, and hence the possibilities for intellectual creativity. Similarly, the rise of popular publishers and publics for literary philosophy (and for philosophical literature) in nineteenth-century Germany, and even more strongly in twentieth-century France, created new networks and new openings for divisions among philosophers. Collins's description of twentieth-century France is similar in many of its details to Casanova's, with many of the same authors (above all Jean-Paul Sartre) playing a leading role in both their histories. However, Collins's attention to networks and personal ties focuses his analysis on the local and national and away from the global competition for prestige, which is the central dynamic in Casanova's analysis.

Casanova and Collins should not be seen as having opposed theories. Rather, they examine two different intellectual fields, so it is not surprising that they uncover different dynamics. Indeed, their methods are complementary: Collins shows how intellectual innovation and debate are built up from the micro-level, and therefore his approach is best suited for tracing the ways in which macro-changes in political economy, states, religion, and public audiences affect philosophical disputation. Casanova is concerned mainly with the dynamics of an entire global field of literary production and reputational ranking. She looks at how individual authors who identify with or in opposition to national literatures advance both personal and collective interests even as external factors play a limited role in altering the dynamics of what she presents as a single, albeit uneven and unequal, world system for the production of literature and literary prestige.

Collins and Casanova both have written enormously ambitious works that are products of decades of reading and analysis. It is not necessary to labor on that scale to produce worthwhile contributions to the historical sociology of culture, or to bring cultural analysis into historical sociology of the state, class, or other topics. However, it is essential to recognize, as Collins and Casanova do, that cultural perceptions and creations occupy places in historically contingent chains. The first step in explaining how a cultural work is produced or how culture is understood and lived is to place that product or that perception in historical context. Only then is it possible to produce a dynamic analysis of the interactions of culture and structure, of perception and action, that Adams, Clemens, and Orloff see as characteristic of the best works of historical sociology's third wave, and which are fulfilled in the other works we have examined in this chapter.

9
Predicting the Future

The techniques of building contingent historical analyses, which are employed by the best works we examined in the previous chapters, can also be used to construct counterfactual histories that allow us to gauge more precisely the causal power of different social forces. Such counterfactual analyses, in turn, can be used to make careful predictions about future change and to specify how possible future developments (such as population increase, global warming, technological innovation, or shifts in global power) will affect states, social movements, culture, family, and gender. In other words, historical sociological analyses can be turned to study the future.

Counterfactual history is an increasingly popular intellectual parlor game, one that unfortunately often is played with little attention to the social forces and constraints that actually determine the outcomes of wars, political conflicts, or other turning points in history. However, "Thinking about unrealized possibilities is an indispensible part of the historian's [and the historical sociologist's] craft – we can judge the forces that prevailed only by comparing them with those that were defeated. All historians, whenever they make causal judgments, are engaging in speculation, are envisioning alternative developments, even when these alternatives are not stated explicitly" (Logevall 1999, p. 395).

We saw Wallerstein ([1986] 2000) undertake just that sort of analysis in chapter 1 when he asked what would have happened if France had succeeded in colonizing southern India. He suggested that India, as a political unit, national identity, and historical topic, would instead have been two countries, which historians would have assumed had distinct cultures and trajectories since before their colonization. Wallerstein used that counterfactual to show that national identity followed rather than preceded the formation (often through colonization and subsequent resistance to foreign rule) of a state.

Zeitlin (1984), whom we discussed in chapter 2, is an example of how to use counterfactual analysis to determine the causal power of different variables. He explains Chile's relative lack of economic development, and relegation to the semi-periphery of the world economy, as the result of industrial capitalists' defeat in two civil wars. Zeitlin makes a counterfactual argument to support his conclusion by identifying the policies the losers in those civil wars would have adopted had they held power, and the consequences of those policies for Chile's development. He uses counterfactual analysis to show that, had the civil wars turned out differently, Chile had the potential to become a core capitalist economy. This allows him to conclude that domestic class forces and the outcome of their civil war, rather than Chile's pre-existing position in the world system, formed the decisive factor in shaping Chile's socioeconomic development.

We need to remember that Zeitlin's analysis, like any precise counterfactual history, is temporally specific. He argues that the opportunity for a different path of economic development was open for Chile only at certain historical moments. Once bourgeois forces were defeated in both civil wars, the opportunity for the country to rise beyond its semi-peripheral position in the world economy was lost for at least a century. (Whether Chile now or in the near future can become an advanced economy is a question that cannot be answered through Zeitlin's nineteenth-century counterfactual.) Zeitlin does suggest that his counterfactual analysis of Chile is a challenge to world systems theory more broadly – that he undermines the determinism of world systems theory by showing this single instance of alternative possibilities. He is able to make such a broad theoretical claim precisely because his historical analysis is so carefully drawn to identify specific key turning points and thereby the causal forces that matter.

Most commonly, counterfactual history is used to advance or to challenge the great man theory of history, by speculating what would have happened if Alexander the Great had lived to age sixty-nine instead of dying as he did at thirty-three (Toynbee 1969), or if Ulysses Grant had died in May, 1863, before he could lead the Union to its decisive victories (Kantor 1961), or if John F. Kennedy had not been assassinated and had lived to serve out two terms as president (Kunz 1997; Logevall 1999). The problem with most great man hypotheticals is that they assert that, rather than analyze how, a single leader could have overcome structural impediments to social change, or argue that a leader's personal flaws prevented an otherwise likely outcome without evaluating the causal importance of other factors. For example, Toynbee hypothesizes that Alexander, through force of personality and strategic genius, could have built and held together an empire encompassing all of Asia and the Middle East, thereby overcoming ethnic and national identities, and consequently undermining the bases for future wars. Toynbee's hypothetical is unsociological in that he ignores the infrastructural limitations of ancient polities that in fact made it impossible for empires like Alexander's to sustain the militaries or administrations needed to build a cohesive polity.

Similarly, Kantor's focus on a single general ignores the fact that the Confederacy by 1863 was suffering from declining morale, mass desertion, and lack of supplies. Even a Southern victory at Gettysburg could not have sufficiently revived morale and overcome the material lacks of the Confederate troops. Placing one man's generalship over the diverging organizational and material endowments of the two armies ignores the factors that actually determine the outcomes of wars. Toynbee and Kantor's counterfactuals are merely extended fantasies and, unlike Zeitlin's work, do not advance our understanding of the causal forces that determine outcomes at specific historical moments, and therefore are not useful for drawing generalizations about social change.

Kunz and Logevall address the same counterfactual question: If President John Kennedy had not been assassinated, would he have sent combat troops to Vietnam and "Americanized" the war? The two scholars give very different answers; however, in the process of constructing their divergent counterfactuals, they advance our understanding of the factors that must be examined to delineate the limits of an individual president's control over US foreign policy. Vietnam, in Kunz's analysis, is another demonstration of the limits of any individual leader's political autonomy. Johnson, as we now know from Oval Office recordings, recollections of aides, and documents, was torn between his fears that escalation would end in disaster and his conviction that the "loss" of Vietnam would result in his defeat in 1964 or his impeachment afterwards. Kennedy, who was elected president in 1960 on a platform of Cold War militarism and accusations of a phony "missile gap," would, in Kunz's view, have faced equally severe political consequences if he had tried to withdraw from Vietnam after being re-elected in 1964. In Kunz's analysis, US presidents have only a limited capacity to change public opinion, which then was firmly committed to an aggressive anti-communist foreign policy, or to challenge the long-standing interests and bureaucratic power of key groups, above all the military, that sought to block any rollback of US commitments abroad.

Logevall focuses his attention on the actual decision-making process of presidents and their advisors. Unlike Kunz, he finds much more opposition to sending US troops to Vietnam among officials within the executive branch and in Congress. Logevall, based on his analysis of statements and positions papers from politicians and officials in the crucial years 1963 to 1965, contends that either Kennedy or Johnson could have decided to withdraw from Vietnam, even though that would have resulted in a communist victory, without provoking great resistance from the US military, State Department, or Congress. Logevall assumes that confidential documents or public statements were accurate reflections of actors' actual views and therefore predict the political positions they would have taken in reaction to subsequent events. Kunz takes a different approach, projecting hypothetical future public positions as reflections of long-standing political and institutional interests, and therefore reaches the opposite conclusion.

Taken together, Logevall and Kunz's opposed counterfactuals clearly do not resolve the questions of what Kennedy would have done about Vietnam in a second term and whether Johnson was the instigator of the war or a largely passive victim of geopolitical forces set in motion well before he became president. However, these two authors do serve to highlight the factors that should be at the center of research on the origins of the US war in Vietnam specifically, and US foreign policy-making in general. Thanks to Kunz, we see the need to clarify how and to what extent public opinion affects policy decisions. Her assertion that neither Kennedy nor Johnson could have turned away from the war shows the necessity of clarifying the steps and causal direction of the interaction between presidential advocacy, policy-making, policy implementation, and public opinion. Logevall's counterfactual identifies the importance of determining how conflicting elite interests and institutional demands result in policy, and how and when presidents are able to exploit divisions among such interests to pursue their own favored policies. These two counterfactuals clarify but don't resolve the fundamental question of what was the relative weight of a president's own preferences, public opinion, and elite and institutional interests in making policy. However, if we are able in the future to resolve that question for the Vietnam War, we will gain analytical leverage in addressing and resolving similar questions about policy decisions at other moments in US history and also create a rubric for posing similar questions about decision-making in other states.

Most turning points in history, as we have seen throughout this book, are not the result of individual leaders' decisions. Rather, historical change is created by contingent series of actions by multiple actors, often combined with conjunctures of events outside of any human actor's control, such as economic or demographic cycles. Counterfactuals can allow us to see if other options in fact were open to actors at key turning points. By tracing out the implications of those alternative choices, we can be more precise about the magnitude of that initial turning point. At the end of chapter 3, we examined Markoff's (1996b) work on the French Revolution. He showed that the National Assembly's decision to abolish feudalism was not an obvious response to clear demands from peasants in revolt. Rather, the Assembly responded to unclear signals, and their legislation was not terribly successful at quieting the peasantry. Markoff does not detail other possible legislative responses; nor does he explore the implications of such different policies for the later political or socioeconomic development of France. Yet, his careful and detailed analysis of peasant grievances, the dynamics of popular protests, and the internal politics of the National Assembly provides the bases to construct such a counterfactual. Of course, those alternative paths were not taken; however, by tracing out the implications of such policies we would be able to specify more precisely how the actual decisions served to limit the room for later agency by peasants and other actors, while opening opportunities for those who sent France down a set of tracks that led in a very different direction from that which would have been created by alternate legislative responses to peasant uprisings.

Barrington Moore (1978, pp. 376–97) provides a model of how to identify feasible alternative political paths and then to construct an argument about the consequences of grasping those unexplored openings. Moore argues that Germany's defeat in World War I and the worker uprising at the war's end so weakened the old regime that the German Social Democratic Party did not need to make the compromises it in fact made with the army and other elites. Objective conditions already existed for the formation of a liberal socialist state that could have had the strength to counter the Nazi challenge a decade later. "The Social Democrats in 1918 had a choice and an opportunity. They neither saw it nor took it because their historical experience had rendered them incapable of doing so" (ibid., p. 394). Moore's exercise in counterfactual history allows him to specify the role that party leaders played in shaping the German state, and to identify the biographical and historical factors that made those leaders blind to the actual possibilities open to them. Moore's great contribution, and what should be one of the principal goals of counterfactual history, is not just to explore alternatives but to identify the factors that made contemporaries blind to, or unwilling to take, those different, and potentially more fruitful, paths.

Counterfactuals are similar to the negative case analyses (Emigh 1997a) we saw in earlier chapters or John Stuart Mills's "method of difference," which "contrast cases in which the phenomena to be explained and the hypothesized causes are present to other ('negative') cases in which the phenomena and causes are both absent, although they are as similar as possible to the 'positive' cases in other respects" (Skocpol and Somers 1980, p. 183). These methods all ask why factors that could have led to a particular outcome (capitalism in Renaissance Tuscany, a stable social democratic government in post-World War I Germany, or social revolutions in England or Japan) did not occur. Similarly, cross-temporal analysis is a way to show how something (the transition to capitalism, the institution of social programs such as universal health insurance in the Untied States) may not occur for a long time, but then suddenly comes about. In these cases we are not engaged in counterfactual analysis, since the event occurs; but we are able to see what changed right before the event and in that way identify the causes or the sequence of contingent events that produced the outcome.

Forecasting future change can be understood as prospective counterfactual history. When done with analytical rigor, prediction allows us to trace the effects of specific changes upon other aspects of social structure and to specify how those changes open or close opportunities for further agency. Let me illustrate with a brief look at three fundamental transformations now occurring that I highlighted at the start of this book: (1) global warming, (2) the decline of work, and (3) the simultaneous rise in inequality in Western nations and declining gap between those nations and some, once poor countries in the rest of the world. My goal here is not actually to predict the consequences of each of those changes; that would require a book in itself. Rather, my aim is to specify the tasks required for such analyses, and to show that they are parallel to those undertaken in the best works of historical sociology we examined in the previous chapters.

Global warming, combined with a projected 50 percent increase in world population over the twenty-first century, will create worldwide shortages of food, water, and other resources, render parts of the globe unlivable, and cause migration on an unprecedented scale as people flee drought- and flood-stricken areas in search of habitable land and other necessities of life. How will those changes affect social structure, and for whom will they open or close opportunities for effective action? If we want to understand the consequences of this coming reality, we first need to identify affected groups and then predict their reactions. Since global warming will affect some regions of the world more heavily than others, we need to examine how different classes, regions, or nation-states would respond to the particular ways in which they will be affected by ecological crisis.

Temporality is as important as physical and social geography. Global warming will not be reversed. Rather, the physical reality of shortages and ecological disasters will continue and intensify (although the shortages could be relieved by catastrophic population declines). However, the social order upon which that physical reality will impact will itself change over time. It is vital to plot out the disruptive changes and social responses step by step, to build contingent chains of change just as historical sociologists have done for past events.

If, for example, the first effect of global warming is to cause mass migrations, then we would need to gauge the effects of such migrations on the states where the refugees would land. Would those states be weakened by the influx of people or would anger by locals against immigrants increase nationalism and strengthen those states' capacities to repel refugees? Similarly, all states will not suffer equally from resource shortages. Would resource-rich states be able to leverage their advantages, or would they become targets of attack? Would those states' capacities change over time, and, if so, how? Would resource-poor states with powerful militaries be able to seize resources from weaker states? Predicting the future requires more than merely answering those questions. In addition, we must trace the ways in which initial changes, such as whether people seeking or trying to protect resources mobilize along class, ethnic, or national lines, or fail to organize themselves at all, shape their later capacities as well as various institutions' subsequent strategies and capacities to take effective action.

When we attempt to answer these questions we are engaged in a prospective counterfactual, evaluating how state policies and capacities, and nations' economies, demographics, and collective identities, would be changed by an altered variable – in this case, global warming and its consequences. Our answers allow us to weigh the power of causal forces in specific situations: for example, to determine how migration affects national identity, the degree to which nationalism shapes state policies, and the efficacy of military power in securing and guarding natural resources.

James Mahoney's (2010) analysis of how the Spanish conquest of America affected social relations and subsequent economic development, which we examined in chapter 4, offers a model of how to undertake the step-by-step prospective analysis of the social consequences of global warming we just outlined. Remember, Mahoney began with a study of the different pre-conquest social structures in the Americas. Similarly, projections about the effects of global warming would need to begin by assessing the organizational and mobilization capacities of institutions and actors prior to ecological crisis. Just as Mahoney traced institutional change from one stage to the next, and sought to identify key events that shifted particular Latin American states off the path-dependent development set by the combination of pre-Columbian social structure and the different eras of Spanish colonial policy, so too would we need to identify events (wars, revolutions, state collapses, shifts in the structure of the world economy) that would pull states, classes, and other actors off the path set by their initial response to ecological catastrophe.

The decline of work, as service jobs follow manufacturing and agriculture in being replaced by machines (Collins forthcoming; Brynjolfssom and McAfee 2012), will not increase unemployment equally across classes and nations. States will vary, as they already do, in their capacity to compensate for lack of jobs in capitalist enterprises by creating public-sector jobs, providing government support for early retirement, or keeping young people in school later into their lives. At the same time, the unemployed and underemployed will respond in different ways to their plight, as those in poverty and without jobs have done in the past. Those responses can range from passive resignation (often accompanied by alcohol and drug use and/or violence turned on one's self, family, and community) to political demands for aid and jobs, which can be directed at different targets (private employers, the local or national state, or other ethnic, national, or religious groups seen as competitors for employment).

If, when, and where the unemployed succeed in gaining concessions, the very scale of programs designed to create jobs or to provide income support would restructure the overall economy and create new political constituencies to sustain such programs. Thus, to the extent that the unemployed are able to compel solutions to technologically induced (and capitalist-propelled) mass unemployment, the future capacities of the unemployed, workers, capitalists, and state officials to organize themselves, and the lines along which they will divide or cohere, will be changed.

We can look to the historical sociologists who have studied the origins of, and variations among, social welfare programs for models of how to analyze this possible future. Just as those scholars whom we encountered in chapter 5 sought to weigh the relative importance of state capacities, popular mobilization, and capitalist class coherence in determining the differences in social welfare benefits across countries, so too would we need to evaluate those factors, and try to figure out how they would change under conditions of rising mass unemployment. Central to the debate on social benefits is the question of whether and how those benefits, and the overall structure of a social welfare state, become locked in, thereby shaping the introduction of new benefits later on. Esping-Andersen, Skocpol, and others answer that question in different ways; however, they all recognize the need to look at how the institutionalization of social benefits affects state capacities, the organization of politics (including parties, elections, and political ideologies), the structure and culture of households and families, and the overall organization of the economy (which can include its degree of decommodification and its place in the capitalist world system). Similarly, we would need to look at the same set of factors if we want to understand how mass unemployment will affect different societies, and especially to predict what the responses will be and how those responses will then alter politics and social relations later. The social welfare states of today are products of chains of contingent change; the future world of fewer jobs and varying state programs to address mass unemployment also will emerge and be altered in a series of interactions between social actors and structures. Both sides of that relationship must be identified, and their changing identities and capacities must be specified.

The rise in inequality in much of North America and Europe (the 'West') over the past three decades, at the same time as the huge income gap between the West and the rest of the world has begun to close, has the potential, especially when combined with resources shortages and mass unemployment, to reorder identities and shift the lines of social solidarity and conflict within nations. We would first want to identify the social groups that have gained or lost, and will continue to gain or lose, relative position in terms of income and wealth. We would then need to compare countries to see where inequality is widening and narrowing. Once we have such a global comparative picture of changes in inequality, we would be in a position to consider how those changes will affect identities and solidarities.

The approach taken by Shanin, Emigh, and Szelenyi and his colleagues, which we discussed in chapter 6, offers a way to begin a study of the consequences of future changes in the intra- and international dimensions of inequality. They show

how individuals, families, and social groups dealt with sudden shifts in income and wealth. Their work is especially helpful for this problem because they trace the ways in which individual and familial strategies combine to reorder politics and class relations, while at the same time showing how epochal shifts in a society's political economy provokes both individual and collective responses. Yet, their studies are concerned, in Shanin's case, with a single country (Russia) and, in Szelenyi's work, with comparing the internal dynamics of a number of countries, without addressing how shifts in a single country's global position affect class and other group identities and actions within its borders. In other words, their analyses do not address how groups or individuals respond to a double movement of changes within their country and in the world economy.

Wallerstein and Arrighi, whose world systems approach we examined in chapter 2, address the sources and consequences of countries' shifting positions in the world system. Indeed, Arrighi (2007) is concerned precisely with explaining how China's rise to the core of the world system affects class dynamics and the state in the country. His discussion of the internal consequences of US decline is more cursory, and therefore he has less to say about how that decline is affecting American politics. This was the problem with world systems analyses highlighted by Zeitlin: a lack of attention to how, or acknowledgement of the possibility that, internal dynamics can contribute to a country's shifting position in the world system. Thus, we can look to Arrighi to understand China's rise in the world since that state's actions as a rising hegemon are integral to the operation of the world system. Conversely, US decline, or that of lesser core countries, and especially the reaction of groups bearing the brunt of decline, is seen as effect more than cause in world system dynamics. As a result, world systems analysts overlook the possibility that nationalism and state power could be strengthened rather than weakened by ongoing shifts in the global economy, and therefore overlook potential sites where reactions against and responses to inequality might occur. When we try to predict the consequences of intra- or international changes in inequality we need to look beyond the immediate consequences for those who gain or lose position, as would status attainment researchers. We also need to be open to the possibility that eventful change begins at sites remote from where inequality is being exacerbated or alleviated.

The lesson we should take away from our examination of comparative historical sociology is that we must focus each study of change, whether historical or prospective, on looking for the moments and sites of effective action. Often those are found at a distance from the sites of existing power and outside the central dynamics that are producing the main events of the moment. The path from cause to effect is often long and almost always contingent. It is the task for comparative historical sociologists to follow that path. That is what the best work on the origins of states, capitalism, and social benefits have done. That is the way we have come to understand the formation, development, and consequences of empires, social movements, and revolutions. It is how we have gained a fuller understanding of historical changes in gender, families, and the cultural frameworks through which social beings think and act. And this is the approach that will allow us to offer rigorous predictions on how environmental disaster, technological change, geopolitical shifts, the growing capacity of those with wealth and power to extend their advantage, or unexpected mobilizations by popular forces will set off chains of cause and effect that might end in unexpected and unanticipated places.

Historical sociology does not have a particular subject matter. Rather, it is a way of doing sociology that recognizes change as the true subject of the discipline. We have seen throughout this book that change and its causes can be explained using a variety of methods: counterfactual history, case studies, negative case, cross-temporal, and cross-national analyses. The best method depends on the problem being studied and the theoretical questions being engaged. Regardless of the method used, the best works share a sensitivity to temporality, an understanding that when something occurs – its place in a sequence of events – is crucial to explaining causality.

Over the two centuries since Marx, Weber, Durkheim, and their contemporaries created this discipline, numerous scholars – from sociology and other fields – have succeeded in providing more precise and richer explanations for a range of historical changes while bringing temporal depth to the often static ways in which problems are framed in many of the subfields of sociology. The techniques and sensibilities of historical sociology are available for rethinking understandings of old problems and for addressing unstudied and understudied moments of social change past, present, and future.

Notes

1   Delanty and Isin (2003, p. 1) see that one of historical sociology's "defining characteristics is a concern with the formation and transformation of modernity." My point is that for its founders that was *the* defining characteristic of *all* of sociology.

2   Some authors have proposed typologies of narrative types, from which sociologists can pick one appropriate for the problem they wish to address. Aminzade (1992) and Stryker (1996), exemplars of this approach, unfortunately pitch their articles at such a general level that they offer little guidance for sociologists or historians as they try to determine how to order evidence from a particular case or cases into explanations of historical change that can form the basis for reaching theoretical generalizations. At the other extreme, historian Lawrence Stone (1979) argues that efforts to "produce generalized laws to explain historical change" (p. 5) are doomed to failure and therefore historians should return to narrative, which he defines as "the organization of material in a chronologically sequential order and the focusing of the content into a single coherent story, albeit with sub-plots" (p. 3). Stone's approach might yield compelling accounts of single events, but those accounts do not provide a basis for comparison or for reaching theoretical generalizations – goals that Stone sees as foolish and unattainable. Hobsbawm (1980) and Abrams (1980) offer rejoinders to Stone's pessimism. In the rest of this chapter and throughout this book I will present works of historical sociology that point to a middle path between generalizations so broad that they

encompass all historical accounts and accounts that are designed, and praised, for their uniqueness and resistance to generalization.

3   Abrams (1982, pp. 201–26) offers an extended comparison of the ways in which historians and sociologists try to explain revolutions.

4   Wallerstein used this passage as the epigraph to the first volume of his *The Modern World-System* (1974).

5   The debate between Dobb and Sweezy and other participants is reprinted in Hilton (1976). Most of the contributors support and elaborate Dobb's position, with Kohachiro Takahashi discussing the application of Dobb's argument to Japanese feudalism as well. Brenner (1976) revived the debate. Brenner's original piece, replies from critics, and his response are reprinted in Aston and Philpin (1985).

6   My purpose in this chapter is not to offer a comprehensive survey of research on revolution or social movements. Rather, I have selected some exemplary studies to show how historical sociologists can construct definitions, theories, and data sets to answer the key questions about revolutions and social movements. Two wonderful books I have not included are Wickham-Crowley (1991) and Foran (2005). The first chapters in both of those books contain valuable overviews of the literature on revolutions. Other useful overviews of the vast literature on revolutions are presented in Foran (1997), chapters 1 and 2, and the concluding chapter of Skocpol (1994).

7   The classic formulations of this perspective include Crane Brinton, *The Anatomy of Revolution* ([1938] 1965), Forrest Colburn, *The Vogue of Revolution in Poor Countries* (1994), Ted Robert Gurr, *Why Men Rebel* (1970), and James Davies's (1962) theory of rising expectations.

8   Paige (1997) widens his analysis to explain how class relations in agrarian export sectors interacted with national politics in Central America to produce divergent outcomes: revolution in Nicaragua, a sustained though unsuccessful revolutionary movement in El Salvador, and social democracy in Costa Rica.

9   As with revolutions, I do not offer an overview of social movement theory here. Snow et al. (2004) is the best entry into the main theoretical traditions and debates over social movements.

10   Anderson's argument has been critiqued by Latin Americanists for giving too much autonomy to culture. His critics point out that ideas of nation continued to shift in the course of struggles for independence and then in post-independence political conflicts, and that national identities were in large part hierarchical

and reflected extreme inequalities in economic and political power, and were further transformed by US dominance in the twentieth century. (Miller 2006 offers a clear overview of these critiques of Anderson.)

11   Calhoun (2006) offers a wonderful overview of Bourdieu's experience in, and writings about, Algeria, and analyzes how Algeria affected the latter's theory and method after his return to France and for the rest of his life.

12   Readers will note that the causal sequence I present here is shorter and simpler than my description of Anderson in chapter 2. That is because in chapter 2 I was analyzing how Anderson constructed an explanation of the transition from feudalism to capitalism. Here we are concerned just with the part of his argument that explains state formation.

13   We examined how Tilly and others addressed that relationship in chapter 3.

14   Loveman (1999) offers an extended critique of Marx.

15   Keister and Moller (2000) is the best review of the dismal state of US research on wealth. Keister herself (2000, 2005) is the US sociologist who has paid the most attention to the distribution of wealth, which she has shown to be much more unequal than that of income in the US, but her focus is mainly on differences among middle strata rather than on the top few percent who hold the vast bulk of income-producing wealth (as opposed to homes, automobiles, and household goods). As a result, she is most interested in identifying individual characteristics, such as education, culture, race, and gender, which correlate with wealth, rather than in identifying the social forces that have intensified the concentration of wealth since the 1970s.

16   Bearman and Deane (1992), whose work we discuss below, identify problems with how other scholars have dealt with historical data on income and occupation. Many of the more comprehensive efforts to trace changes in the distribution of wealth and income in historical societies have been made by economists rather than sociologists or historians. Notable examples are Williamson and Lindert (1980), who present what data exist for the distribution of income and wealth in the US from the colonial period to the twentieth century; Herlihy and Klapisch-Zuber (1978), historians who analyze a fourteenth-century Florentine survey of wealth; and Milanovic (2011), an economist who provides a broad overview of inequality through human history and offers varied measures to compare the degree of inequality over millennia.

17   Emigh (1997b) offers an excellent review and critique of this literature.

18 See Lachmann (2006) for a symposium in which nine authors critique Adams et al.'s essay and present their own understandings of the history of US historical sociology.

19 Bakhtin's book raises the question of how he was able to perceive the historical bases of Rabelais and the original meaning of carnival and the grotesque. Bakhtin, modestly, does not offer an answer; however, one is implicit in the logic of his analysis. If the original meaning of carnival and grotesque came from a pre-class society, or at least a society in which class lines were open to challenge, then Bakhtin, by living and writing in the early Soviet Union, when class power again was challenged and an alternative society seemed under construction, gained the perspective to recover similar possibilities in Rabelais' carnival and grotesque.

20 See Collins (2000) for his forty-five page précis of this thousand-page book.

References

Aaronson, Daniel, and Bhashkar Mazumder (2007) "Intergenerational Economic Mobility in the U.S., 1940 to 2000," Federal Reserve Bank of Chicago, www.chicagofed.org/digital_assets/publications/working_papers/2005/wp2005_12.pdf (retrieved August 7, 2012).

Abbott, Andrew (1992) "What Do Cases Do? Some Notes on Activity in Sociological Analysis," pp. 53–82 in *What is a Case? Exploring the Foundations of Social Inquiry*, ed. Charles C. Ragin and Howard Saul Becker. Cambridge: Cambridge University Press.

Abrams, Philip (1980) "History, Sociology, Historical Sociology," *Past & Present*, no. 87: 3–16.

Abrams, Philip (1982) *Historical Sociology*. Shepton Mallet, Somerset: Open Books.

Adams, Julia (2005) *The Familial State: Ruling Families and Merchant Capitalism in Early Modern Europe*. Ithaca, NY: Cornell University Press.

Adams, Julia, Elisabeth Clemens, and Ann Shola Orloff (2005) *Remaking Modernity: Politics, History, and Sociology*. Durham, NC: Duke University Press.

Aminzade, Ronald (1992) "Historical Sociology and Time," *Sociological Methods and Research*, 20: 456–80.

Anderson, Benedict ([1983] 1991) *Imagined Communities: Reflections on the Origin and Spread of Nationalism*. London: Verso.

Anderson, Perry (1974) *Lineages of the Absolutist State*. London: New Left Books.

Arrighi, Giovanni (1994) *The Long Twentieth Century: Money, Power and the Origins of our Times*. London: Verso.

Arrighi, Giovanni (2007) *Adam Smith in Beijing: Lineages of the Twenty-First Century*. London: Verso.

Aston, T. H., and C. H. E. Philpin (1985) *The Brenner Debate: Agrarian Class Structure and Economic Development in Pre-Industrial Europe*. Cambridge: Cambridge University Press.

Aymard, Maurice (1982) "From Feudalism to Capitalism in Italy: The Case that Doesn't Fit," *Review*, 6(2): 131–208.

Bakhtin, Mikhail ([1965] 1968) *Rabelais and his World*. Cambridge, MA: MIT Press.

Barkey, Karen (2008) *Empire of Difference: The Ottomans in Comparative Perspective*. Cambridge: Cambridge University Press.

Barkey, Karen, and Mark von Hagen, eds (2008) *After Empire: Multiethnic Societies and Nation-Building: The Soviet Union and the Russian, Ottoman and Habsburg Empires*. Boulder CO: Westview Press.

Bearman, Peter S., and Glenn Deane (1992) "The Structure of Opportunity: Middle Class Mobility in England, 1548–1689," *American Journal of Sociology*, 98(1): 30–66.

Becker, Jaime, and Jack A. Goldstone (2005) "How Fast Can You Build a State? State Building in Revolutions," pp. 183–210 in *States and Development: Historical Antecedents of Stagnation and Advance*, ed. Matthew Lange and Dietrich Rueschemeyer. New York: Palgrave Macmillan.

Berkner, Lutz K. (1978) "Inheritance, Land Tenure and Peasant Family Structure: A German Regional Comparison," pp. 71–95 in *Family and Inheritance: Rural Society in Western Europe, 1200–1800*, ed. Jack Goody, Joan Thirsk, and Edward Thompson. New York: Cambridge University Press.

Bourdieu, Pierre (1958) *Sociologie d'Algerie*. Paris: PUF.

Braudel, Fernand (1977) *Afterthoughts on Material Civilization and Capitalism*. Baltimore: Johns Hopkins University Press.

Breiger, Ronald (1990) "Introduction: On the Structural Analysis of Social Mobility," pp. 1–23 in *Social Mobility and Social Structure*, ed. Ronald Breiger. Cambridge: Cambridge University Press.

Brenner, Robert (1976) "Agrarian Class Structure and Economic Development in Pre-Industrial Europe," *Past & Present*, no. 70: 30–75.

Brenner, Robert (1982) "The Agrarian Roots of European Capitalism," *Past & Present*, no. 97: 16–113.

Breslin, Jimmy (1990) *Table Money*. New York: Random House.

Brinton, Crane ([1938] 1965) *The Anatomy of Revolution*. New York: Vintage.

Brynjolfssom, Erik, and Andrew McAfee (2012) *Race against the Machine: How the Digital Revolution is Accelerating Innovation,*

Driving Productivity, and Irreversibly Transforming Employment and the Economy. Cambridge, MA: Digital Frontier Press.

Burke, Peter (2003) "The Annales, Braudel and Historical Sociology," pp. 58–64 in *Handbook of Historical Sociology*, ed. Gerard Delanty and Engin F. Isin. London: Sage.

Calhoun, Craig (2003) "Afterword: Why Historical Sociology?," pp. 383–93 in *Handbook of Historical Sociology*, ed. Gerard Delanty and Engin F. Isin. London: Sage.

Calhoun, Craig (2006) "Pierre Bourdieu and Social Transformation: Lessons from Algeria," *Development and Change*, 37(6): 1403–15.

Casanova, Pascale ([1999] 2004) *The World Republic of Letters.* Cambridge, MA: Harvard University Press.

Chakrabarty, Dipesh (2007) *Provincializing Europe: Postcolonial Thought and Historical Difference.* Princeton, NJ: Princeton University Press.

Charlesworth, Andrew, ed. (1983) *An Atlas of Rural Protest in Britain, 1548–1900.* Philadelphia: University of Pennsylvania Press.

Charrad, Mounira M. (2001) *States and Women's Rights: The Making of Postcolonial Tunisia, Algeria, and Morocco.* Berkeley: University of California Press.

Colburn, Forrest (1994) *The Vogue of Revolution in Poor Countries.* Princeton, NJ: Princeton University Press.

Collins, Randall (1980) "Weber's Last Theory of Capitalism: A Systematization," *American Sociological Review*, 45: 925–42.

Collins, Randall (1998) *The Sociology of Philosophies: A Global Theory of Intellectual Change.* Cambridge, ma: Harvard University Press.

Collins, Randall (2000) "The Sociology of Philosophies: A Précis," *Philosophy of the Social Sciences*, 30(2): 158–201.

Collins, Randall (forthcoming) "Technological Displacement of Middle-Class Work and the Long-term Crisis of Capitalism: No More Escapes," In *Does Capitalism Have a Future?*, ed. Craig Calhoun and Georgi Derluguian. Cambridge, MA: Harvard University Press.

Davies, James (1962) "Toward a Theory of Revolution," *American Sociological Review*, 27: 5–18.

Davis, Kingsley (1955) "Institutional Patterns Favoring High Fertility in Underdeveloped Areas," *Eugenics Quarterly*, 2: 33–9.

Delanty, Gerard, and Engin F. Isin (2003) "Introduction: Reorienting Historical Sociology," pp. 1–10 in *Handbook of Historical Sociology*, ed. Gerard Delanty and Engin F. Isin. London: Sage.

Delumeau, Jean ([1971] 1977) *Catholicism between Luther and Voltaire.* London: Burns & Oates.

Dobb, Maurice (1947) *Studies in the Development of Capitalism.* New York: International Publishers.

Domhoff, G. William (1986) "Welfare Capitalism and the Social Security Act of 1935," *American Sociological Review,* 51: 445–6.

Dutton, Michael (2005) "The Trick of Words: Asian Studies, Translations, and the Problems of Knowledge," pp. 89–125 in *The Politics of Method in the Human Sciences,* ed. George Steinmetz. Durham, NC: Duke University Press.

Eisenstadt, S. N. (1963) *The Political Systems of Empires.* New York: Free Press.

Eisenstadt, S. N. (1968) "The Protestant Ethic Thesis in an Analytical and Comparative Framework," pp. 3–45 in *The Protestant Ethic and Modernization,* ed. S. N. Eisenstadt. New York: Basic Books.

Elias, Norbert ([1939] 1982) *The Civilizing Process,* 2 vols. New York: Pantheon.

Elias, Norbert ([1969] 1983) *The Court Society.* New York: Pantheon.

Emigh, Rebecca Jean (1997a) "The Power of Negative Thinking: The Use of Negative Case Methodology in the Development of Sociological Theory," *Theory and Society,* 26: 649–84.

Emigh, Rebecca Jean (1997b) "Land Tenure, Household Structure, and Age at Marriage in Fifteenth-Century Tuscany," *Journal of Interdisciplinary History,* 27(4): 613–36.

Emigh, Rebecca Jean (2009) *The Undevelopment of Capitalism: Sectors and Markets in Fifteenth-Century Tuscany.* Philadelphia: Temple University Press.

Epstein, S. R. (1991) "Cities, Regions and the Late Medieval Crisis: Sicily and Tuscany Compared," *Past & Present,* no. 130: 3–50.

Esping-Andersen, Gøsta (1990) *The Three Worlds of Welfare Capitalism.* Princeton, NJ: Princeton University Press.

Esping-Andersen, Gøsta (1999) *Social Foundations of Postindustrial Economies.* New York: Oxford University Press.

Eyal, Gil, Ivan Szelenyi, and Eleanor Townsley (1998) *Making Capitalism without Capitalists: Class Formation and Elite Struggles in Post-Communist Central Europe.* London: Verso.

Foran, John, ed. (1997) *Theorizing Revolutions.* London: Routledge.

Foran, John (2005) *Taking Power: On the Origins of Third World Revolutions.* Cambridge: Cambridge University Press.

Franzosi, Roberto (1995) *The Puzzle of Strikes: Class and State Strategies in Postwar Italy.* Cambridge: Cambridge University Press.

Fulbrook, Mary (1983) *Piety and Politics: Religion and the Rise of Absolutism in England, Wurttemberg and Prussia*. Cambridge: Cambridge University Press.

Go, Julian (2011) *Patterns of Empire: The British and American Empires, 1688 to the Present*. New York: Cambridge University Press.

Goldstone, Jack (1991) *Revolution and Rebellion in the Early Modern World*. Berkeley: University of California Press.

Goldstone, Jack (2010) "The New Population Bomb: Five Population Megatrends that will Shape the coming Global Future," *Foreign Affairs*, 89(1): 31–43.

Goodwin, Jeff (2001) *No Other Way Out: States and Revolutionary Movements, 1945–1991*. Cambridge: Cambridge University Press.

Gorski, Philip (2003) *The Disciplinary Revolution: Calvinism and the Rise of the State in Early Modern Europe*. Chicago: University of Chicago Press.

Gould, Roger V. (1995) *Insurgent Identities: Class, Community, and Protest in Paris from 1848 to the Commune*. Chicago: University of Chicago Press.

Gurr, Ted Robert (1970) *Why Men Rebel*. Princeton, NJ: Princeton University Press.

Haggard, Stephan, and Robert R. Kaufman (2008) *Development, Democracy and Welfare States: Latin America, East Asia, and Eastern Europe*. Princeton, NJ: Princeton University Press.

Hajnal, John (1965) "European Marriage Patterns in Perspective," pp. 101–43 in *Population in History: Essays in Historical Demography*, ed. David Glass and David Eversley. Chicago: Aldine.

Herlihy, David, and Christiane Klapisch-Zuber (1978) *Les Toscans et leurs familles*. Paris: Presses de la Fondation Nationale des Sciences Politiques.

Hill, Christopher (1972) *The World Turned Upside Down*. London: Penguin.

Hilton, Rodney, ed. (1976) *The Transition from Feudalism to Capitalism*. London: New Left Books.

Hobsbawm, Eric (1980) "The Revival of Narrative: Some Comments," *Past & Present*, no. 86: 3–8.

Hung, Ho-fung (2011) *Protest with Chinese Characteristics*. New York: Columbia University Press.

Ikegami, Eiko (1995) *The Taming of the Samurai: Honorific Individualism and the Making of Modern Japan*. Cambridge, MA: Harvard University Press.

Jacobs, Lawrence R., and Theda Skocpol (2010) *Health Care Reform and American Politics: What Everyone Needs to Know*. New York: Oxford University Press.

Jenkins, J. Craig, and Barbara Brents (1989) "Social Protest, Hegemonic Competition and Social Reform: The Political Origins of the American Welfare State," *American Sociological Review*, 54: 891–909.

Kantor, MacKinlay (1961) *If the South Had Won the Civil War*. New York: Bantam Books.

Keister, Lisa A. (2000) *Wealth in America: Trends in Wealth Inequality*. Cambridge: Cambridge University Press.

Keister, Lisa A. (2005) *Getting Rich: America's New Rich and How They Got That Way*. Cambridge: Cambridge University Press.

Keister, Lisa A., and Stephanie Moller (2000) "Wealth Inequality in the United States," *Annual Review of Sociology*, 26: 63–81.

King, Lawrence Peter, and Ivan Szelenyi (2004) *Theories of the New Class: Intellectuals and Power*. Minneapolis: University of Minnesota Press.

Kranz, Linda (2004) *All About Me: A Keepsake Journal for Kids*. Flagstaff, AZ: Rising Moon.

Kumar, Krishan (2003) *The Making of English National Identity*. Cambridge: Cambridge University Press.

Kunz, Diane (1997) "Camelot Continued: What if John F. Kennedy Had Lived?," pp. 368–91 in *Virtual History: Alternatives and Counterfactuals*, ed. Niall Ferguson. New York: Basic Books.

Kuznets, Simon (1955) "Economic Growth and Income Inequality," *American Economic Review*, 45(1): 1–28.

Lachmann, Richard (1987) *From Manor to Market: Structural Change in England, 1536–1640*. Madison: University of Wisconsin Press.

Lachmann, Richard (2000) *Capitalists in Spite of Themselves: Elite Conflict and Economic Transitions in Early Modern Europe*. New York: Oxford University Press.

Lachmann, Richard, ed. (2006) "Symposium on *Remaking Modernity: Politics, History, and Sociology*," *International Journal of Comparative Sociology*, 47(6) [special issue].

Lachmann, Richard (2010) *States and Power*. Cambridge: Polity.

Lefebvre, Georges ([1932] 1973) *The Great Fear of 1789: Rural Panic in Revolutionary France*. New York: Vintage.

Levine, David, and Keith Wrightson (1991) *The Making of an Industrial Society: Whickham, 1560–1765*. Oxford: Clarendon Press.

Levy, Marion J. (1966) *Modernization and the Structure of Societies: A Setting for International Affairs*. Princeton, NJ: Princeton University Press.

Levy, Marion J. (1972) *Modernization: Latecomers and Survivors*. New York: Basic Books.

Logevall, Fredrik (1999) *Choosing War: The Lost Chance for Peace and the Escalation of War in Vietnam*. Berkeley: University of California Press.

Loveman, Mara (1999) "Making 'Race' and Nation in the United States, South Africa, and Brazil: Taking Making Seriously," *Theory and Society*, 28: 903–27.

Mahoney, James (2010) *Colonialism and Postcolonial Development: Spanish America in Comparative Perspective*. Cambridge: Cambridge University Press.

Mann, Michael (1986, 1993, 2012) *The Sources of Social Power*, Vols 1–3. Cambridge: Cambridge University Press.

Markoff, John (1996a) *Waves of Democracy*. Thousand Oaks, CA: Sage.

Markoff, John (1996b) *The Abolition of Feudalism: Peasants, Lords, and Legislators in the French Revolution*. Pittsburgh: Pennsylvania State University Press.

Marx, Anthony W. (1998) *Making Race and Nation: A Comparison of the United States, South Africa, and Brazil*. Cambridge: Cambridge University Press.

Marx, Karl ([1852] 1963) *The Eighteenth Brumaire of Louis Bonaparte*. New York: International Publishers.

Marx, Karl ([1867] 1967) *Capital*, Vol. 1. New York: International Publishers.

McAdam, Doug (1990) *Freedom Summer*. New York: Oxford University Press.

Meyer, John, John Boli, George M. Thomas, and Francisco O. Ramirez (1997) "World Society and the Nation-State," *American Journal of Sociology*, 103(1): 144–81.

Milanovic, Branko (2011) *The Haves and the Have-Nots: A Brief and Idiosyncratic History of Global Inequality*. New York: Basic Books.

Miller, Nicola (2006) "The Historiography of Nationalism and National Identity in Latin America," *Nations and Nationalism*, 12: 201–21.

Moore, Barrington, Jr. (1978) *Injustice: The Social Bases of Obedience and Revolt*. White Plains, NY: Sharpe.

O'Connor, Julia S., Ann Shola Orloff, and Sheila Shaver (1999) *States, Markets, Families: Gender, Liberalism, and Social Policy in Australia, Canada, Great Britain, and the United States*. Cambridge: Cambridge University Press.

Orloff, Ann Shola (1993) "Gender and the Social Rights of Citizenship: The Comparative Analysis of Gender Relations and Welfare States," *American Sociological Review*, 58: 303–28.

Orloff, Ann, and Theda Skocpol (1984) "Why Not Equal Protection: Explaining the Politics of Public Social Spending in Britain, 1900–1911, and the United States, 1880s–1920," *American Sociological Review*, 49: 726–50.

Paige, Jeffery (1975) *Agrarian Revolution: Social Movements and Export Agriculture in the Underdeveloped World*. New York: Free Press.

Paige, Jeffery (1997) *Coffee and Power: Revolution and the Rise of Democracy in Central America*. Cambridge, MA: Harvard University Press.

Piketty, Thomas, and Emmanuel Saez (2007–12) "Income Inequality in the United States, 1913–2002," pp. 141–225 in *Top Incomes over the Twentieth Century: A Contrast between European and English Speaking Countries*, ed. A. B. Atkinson and T. Piketty. Oxford: Oxford University Press, 2007. Tables and Figures updated to 2010 at http://elsa.berkeley.edu/~saez/.

Piven, Frances Fox, and Richard Cloward (1971) *Regulating the Poor: The Functions of Public Welfare*. New York: Vintage.

Prasad, Monica (2006) *The Politics of Free Markets: The Rise of Neoliberal Economic Policies in Britain, France, Germany, and the United States*. Chicago: University of Chicago Press.

Quadagno, Jill (1984) "Welfare Capitalism and the Social Security Act of 1935," *American Sociological Review*, 49: 632–47.

Quadagno, Jill (1985) "Two Models of Welfare State Development: Reply to Skocpol and Amenta," *American Sociological Review*, 50: 575–8.

Quadagno, Jill (1986) "Reply to Domhoff," *American Sociological Review*, 51: 446.

Quadagno, Jill (2004) "Why the United States Has No National Health Insurance: Stakeholder Mobilization against the Welfare State, 1945–1996," *Journal of Health and Social Behavior*, 45: 25–44.

Seccombe, Wally (1992) *A Millennium of Family Change: Feudalism to Capitalism in Northwestern Europe*. London: Verso.

Seccombe, Wally (1993) *Weathering the Storm: Working-Class Families from the Industrial Revolution to the Fertility Decline*. London: Verso.

Sen, Amartya (1992) *Inequality Reexamined*. Cambridge, MA: Harvard University Press.

Sewell, William H., Jr. (1996) "Three Temporalities: Toward an Eventful Sociology," pp. 245–80 in *The Historic Turn in the Human Sciences*, ed. Terrence J. McDonald. Ann Arbor: University of Michigan Press.

Shanin, Teodor (1972) *The Awkward Class*. Oxford: Clarendon Press.

Shapiro, Gilbert, and John Markoff (1998) *Revolutionary Demands: A Content Analysis of the Cahiers de doléances of 1789*. Stanford, CA: Stanford University Press.

Skocpol, Theda (1979) *States and Social Revolutions: A Comparative Analysis of France, Russia, and China*. Cambridge: Cambridge University Press.

Skocpol, Theda (1982) "Rentier State and Shi'a Islam in the Iranian Revolution," *Theory and Society*, 11(3): 265–83.

Skocpol, Theda (1994) *Social Revolutions in the Modern World*. Cambridge: Cambridge University Press.

Skocpol, Theda (1996) *Boomerang: Clinton's Health Security Effort and the Turn against Government in U.S. Politics*. New York: Norton.

Skocpol, Theda, and Edwin Amenta (1985) "Did Capitalists Shape Social Security?," *American Sociological Review*, 50: 572–5.

Skocpol, Theda, and Edwin Amenta (1986) "States and Social Policies," *Annual Review of Sociology*, 12: 131–57.

Skocpol, Theda, and Margaret Somers (1980) "The Uses of Comparative History in Macrosocial Inquiry," *Comparative Studies in Society and History*, 22: 174–97.

Smith, Philip (2005) *Why War? The Cultural Logic of Iraq, the Gulf War, and Suez*. Chicago: University of Chicago Press.

Snow, David A., Sarah A. Soule, and Hanspeter Kriesi, eds (2004) *The Blackwell Companion to Social Movements*. Oxford: Blackwell.

Somers, Margaret (1993) "Citizenship and the Place of the Public Sphere: Law, Community and Political Culture in the Transition to Democracy," *American Sociological Review*, 58: 587–620.

Somers, Margaret (2008) *Genealogies of Citizenship: Markets, Statelessness, and the Right to Have Rights*. Cambridge: Cambridge University Press.

Steinmetz, George (2007) *The Devil's Handwriting: Precoloniality and the German Colonial State in Qingdao, Samoa, and Southwest Africa*. Chicago: University of Chicago Press.

Steinmetz, George (2008) "The Colonial State as a Social Field," *American Sociological Review*, 73: 589–612.

Steinmetz, George, ed. (2012) *Sociology and Empire: Colonial Studies and the Imperial Entanglements of a Discipline*. Durham, NC: Duke University Press.

Stone, Lawrence (1965) *The Crisis of the Aristocracy, 1558–1641*. Oxford: Clarendon Press.

Stone, Lawrence (1977) *The Family, Sex and Marriage in England, 1500–1800*. New York: Harper & Row.

Stone, Lawrence (1979) "The Revival of Narrative: Reflections on a New Old History," *Past & Present*, no. 85: 3–24.

Stone, Lawrence, and Jeanne C. Fawtier Stone (1984) *An Open Elite? England 1540–1880*. Oxford: Clarendon Press.

Stryker, Robin (1996) "Beyond History vs. Theory: Strategic Narrative and Sociological Explanation," *Sociological Methods and Research*, 24: 304–52.

Sweezy, Paul ([1950] 1976) "A Critique," pp. 33–56 in *The Transition from Feudalism to Capitalism*, ed. Rodney Hilton. London: New Left Books.

Tarrow, Sidney (2004) "From Comparative Historical Analysis to 'Local Theory': The Italian City-State Route to the Modern State," *Theory and Society*, 33: 443–71.

Therborn, Goran (2004) *Between Sex and Power: Family in the World, 1900–2000*. London: Routledge.

Therborn, Goran (2006) "Meaning, Mechanisms, Patterns, and Forces: An Introduction," pp. 1–58 in *Inequalities of the World: New Theoretical Frameworks, Multiple Empirical Approaches*, ed. Goran Therborn. London: Verso.

Thernstrom, Stephen (1964) *Poverty and Progress: Social Mobility in a Nineteenth Century City*. Cambridge, MA: Harvard University Press.

Tilly, Charles (1986) *The Contentious French*. Cambridge, MA: Belknap Press of Harvard University Press.

Tilly, Charles (1990) *Coercion, Capital, and European States*. Oxford: Blackwell.

Tilly, Charles (1991) "How and What Are Historians Doing," pp. 86–117 in *Divided Knowledge across Disciplines, across Cultures*, ed. David Easton and Corinne S. Schelling. Newbury Park, CA: Sage.

Tilly, Charles (1993) *European Revolutions, 1492–1992*. Oxford: Blackwell.

Tilly, Charles (1995) *Popular Contention in Great Britain, 1758–1834*. Cambridge, MA: Harvard University Press.

Tilly, Charles (1998) *Durable Inequality*. Berkeley: University of California Press.

Tilly, Charles (2005) *Trust and Rule*. Cambridge: Cambridge University Press.

Tocqueville, Alexis de ([1835] 2003) *Democracy in America*. New York: Penguin.

Toynbee, Arnold (1969) "If Alexander the Great Had Lived On," pp. 441–86 in *Some Problems of Greek History*. London: Oxford University Press.

Wakin, Eric (1998) *Anthropology Goes to War: Professional Ethics and Counterinsurgency in Thailand*. Madison: University of Wisconsin Press.

Wallerstein, Immanuel (1974–2011) *The Modern World System*, Vols 1–4. Berkeley: University of California Press.

Wallerstein, Immanuel ([1986] 2000) "Does India Exist?," pp. 310–14 in *The Essential Wallerstein*. New York: New Press.

Weber, Max ([1916–17] 1958) *The Protestant Ethic and the Spirit of Capitalism*. New York: Scribner's.

Weber, Max ([1922] 1978) *Economy and Society*. Berkeley: University of California Press.

Wickham-Crowley, Timothy (1991) *Guerillas and Revolution in Latin America: A Comparative Study of Insurgents and Regimes since 1956*. Princeton, NJ: Princeton University Press.

Williamson, Jeffrey G., and Peter H. Lindert (1980) *American Inequality: A Macroeconomic History*. New York: Academic Press.

Wrightson, Keith, and David Levine (1979) *Poverty and Piety in an English Village: Terling, 1525–1700*. New York: Academic Press.

Zeitlin, Maurice (1984) *The Civil Wars in Chile, or, The Bourgeois Revolutions that Never Were*. Princeton, NJ: Princeton University Press.

Zhao, Dingxin (2001) *The Power of Tiananmen: State–Society Relations and the 1989 Beijing Student Movement*. Chicago: University of Chicago Press.

Index